LANGUAGE AND LITERACY SERIES

Real World Writing for Secondary Students: Teaching the College Admission Essay and Other Gate-Openers for Higher Education
JESSICA SINGER EARLY & MEREDITH DECOSTA

Teaching Vocabulary to English Language Learners
MICHAEL F. GRAVES, DIANE AUGUST, & JEANNETTE MANCILLA-MARTINEZ

Literacy for a Better World: The Promise of Teaching in Diverse Schools
LAURA SCHNEIDER VANDERPLOEG

Socially Responsible Literacy: Teaching Adolescents for Purpose and Power
PAULA M. SELVESTER & DEBORAH G. SUMMERS

Learning from Culturally and Linguistically Diverse Classrooms: Using Inquiry to Inform Practice
JOAN C. FINGON & SHARON H. ULANOFF, EDS.

Bridging Literacy and Equity
ALTHIER M. LAZAR, PATRICIA A. EDWARDS, & GWENDOLYN THOMPSON MCMILLON

"Trust Me! I Can Read"
SALLY LAMPING & DEAN WOODRING BLASE

Reading Girls
HADAR DUBOWSKY MA'AYAN

Reading Time
CATHERINE COMPTON-LILLY

A Call to Creativity
LUKE REYNOLDS

Literacy and Justice Through Photography
WENDY EWALD, KATHERINE HYDE, & LISA LORD

The Successful High School Writing Center
DAWN FELS & JENNIFER WELLS, EDS.

Interrupting Hate
MOLLIE V. BLACKBURN

Playing Their Way into Literacies
KAREN E. WOHLWEND

Teaching Literacy for Love and Wisdom
JEFFREY D. WILHELM & BRUCE NOVAK

Overtested
JESSICA ZACHER PANDYA

Restructuring Schools for Linguistic Diversity, Second Edition
OFELIA B. MIRAMONTES, ADEL NADEAU, & NANCY L. COMMINS

Words Were All We Had
MARÍA DE LA LUZ REYES, ED.

Urban Literacies
VALERIE KINLOCH, ED.

Bedtime Stories and Book Reports
CATHERINE COMPTON-LILLY & STUART GREENE, EDS.

Envisioning Knowledge
JUDITH A. LANGER

Envisioning Literature, Second Edition
JUDITH A. LANGER

Writing Assessment and the Revolution in Digital Texts and Technologies
MICHAEL R. NEAL

Artifactual Literacies
KATE PAHL & JENNIFER ROWSELL

Educating Emergent Bilinguals
OFELIA GARCÍA & JO ANNE KLEIFGEN

(Re)Imagining Content-Area Literacy Instruction
RONI JO DRAPER, ED.

Change Is Gonna Come
PATRICIA A. EDWARDS, GWENDOLYN THOMPSON MCMILLON, & JENNIFER D. TURNER

When Commas Meet Kryptonite
MICHAEL BITZ

Literacy Tools in the Classroom
RICHARD BEACH, GERALD CAMPANO, BRIAN EDMISTON, & MELISSA BORGMANN

Harlem on Our Minds
VALERIE KINLOCH

Teaching the New Writing
ANNE HERRINGTON, KEVIN HODGSON, & CHARLES MORAN, EDS.

Critical Encounters in High School English, Second Edition
DEBORAH APPLEMAN

Children, Language, and Literacy
CELIA GENISHI & ANNE HAAS DYSON

Children's Language
JUDITH WELLS LINDFORS

The Administration and Supervision of Reading Programs, Fourth Edition
SHELLEY B. WEPNER & DOROTHY S. STRICKLAND, EDS.

"You Gotta BE the Book," Second Edition
JEFFREY D. WILHELM

No Quick Fix
RICHARD L. ALLINGTON & SEAN A. WALMSLEY, EDS.

Children's Literature and Learning
BARBARA A. LEHMAN

Storytime
LARWRENCE R. SIPE

Effective Instruction for Struggling Readers, K–6
BARBARA M. TAYLOR & JAMES E. YSSELDYKE, EDS.

The Effective Literacy Coach
ADRIAN RODGERS & EMILY M. RODGERS

Writing in Rhythm
MAISHA T. FISHER

Reading the Media
RENEE HOBBS

teaching**media**_literacy_.com
RICHARD BEACH

What Was It Like?
LINDA J. RICE

(continued)

For volumes in the NCRLL Collection (edited by JoBeth Allen and Donna E. Alvermann) and the Practitioners Bookshelf Series (edited by Celia Genishi and Donna E. Alvermann), please visit www.tcpress.com.

Once Upon a Fact
CAROL BRENNAN JENKINS & ALICE EARLE

Research on Composition
PETER SMAGORINSKY, ED.

Critical Literacy/Critical Teaching
CHERYL DOZIER, PETER JOHNSTON, & REBECCA ROGERS

The Vocabulary Book
MICHAEL F. GRAVES

Building on Strength
ANA CELIA ZENTELLA, ED.

Powerful Magic
NINA MIKKELSEN

New Literacies in Action
WILLIAM KIST

Teaching English Today
BARRIE R.C. BARRELL ET AL., EDS.

Bridging the Literacy Achievement Gap, 4–12
DOROTHY S. STRICKLAND & DONNA E. ALVERMANN, EDS.

Crossing the Digital Divide
BARBARA MONROE

Out of This World
HOLLY VIRGINIA BLACKFORD

Critical Passages
KRISTIN DOMBEK & SCOTT HERNDON

Making Race Visible
STUART GREENE & DAWN ABT-PERKINS, EDS.

The Child as Critic, Fourth Edition
GLENNA SLOAN

Room for Talk
REBEKAH FASSLER

Give Them Poetry!
GLENNA SLOAN

The Brothers and Sisters Learn to Write
ANNE HAAS DYSON

"Just Playing the Part"
CHRISTOPHER WORTHMAN

The Testing Trap
GEORGE HILLOCKS, JR.

Reading Lives
DEBORAH HICKS

Inquiry Into Meaning
EDWARD CHITTENDEN & TERRY SALINGER, WITH ANNE M. BUSSIS

"Why Don't They Learn English?"
LUCY TSE

Conversational Borderlands
BETSY RYMES

Inquiry-Based English Instruction
RICHARD BEACH & JAMIE MYERS

The Best for Our Children
MARÍA DE LA LUZ REYES & JOHN J. HALCÓN, EDS.

Language Crossings
KAREN L. OGULNICK, ED.

What Counts as Literacy?
MARGARET GALLEGO & SANDRA HOLLINGSWORTH, EDS.

Beginning Reading and Writing
DOROTHY S. STRICKLAND & LESLEY M. MORROW, EDS.

Reading for Meaning
BARBARA M. TAYLOR, MICHAEL F. GRAVES,
& PAUL VAN DEN BROEK, EDS.

Young Adult Literature and the New Literary Theories
ANNA O. SOTER

Literacy Matters
ROBERT P. YAGELSKI

Children's Inquiry
JUDITH WELLS LINDFORS

Close to Home
JUAN C. GUERRA

Life at the Margins
JULIET MERRIFIELD ET AL.

Literacy for Life
HANNA ARLENE FINGERET & CASSANDRA DRENNON

The Book Club Connection
SUSAN I. MCMAHON & TAFFY E. RAPHAEL, EDS., ET AL.

Until We Are Strong Together
CAROLINE E. HELLER

Writing Superheroes
ANNE HAAS DYSON

Opening Dialogue
MARTIN NYSTRAND ET AL.

Just Girls
MARGARET J. FINDERS

The First R
MICHAEL F. GRAVES, PAUL VAN DEN BROEK, &
BARBARA M. TAYLOR, EDS.

Talking Their Way into Science
KAREN GALLAS

The Languages of Learning
KAREN GALLAS

Partners in Learning
CAROL LYONS, GAY SU PINNELL, & DIANE DEFORD

Social Worlds of Children Learning to Write
in an Urban Primary School
ANNE HAAS DYSON

Inside/Outside
MARILYN COCHRAN-SMITH & SUSAN L. LYTLE

Whole Language Plus
COURTNEY B. CAZDEN

Learning to Read
G. BRIAN THOMPSON & TOM NICHOLSON, EDS.

Engaged Reading
JOHN T. GUTHRIE & DONNA E. ALVERMANN

REAL WORLD WRITING for SECONDARY STUDENTS

Teaching the College Admission Essay and Other Gate-Openers for Higher Education

JESSICA SINGER EARLY
MEREDITH DECOSTA

Foreword by Charles Bazerman

Teachers College, Columbia University
New York and London

National Writing Project
Berkeley, California

Published simultaneously by Teachers College Press, 1234 Amsterdam Avenue, New York, NY 10027 and National Writing Project, 2105 Bancroft Way, Berkeley, CA 94720-1042

The National Writing Project (NWP) is a nationwide network of educators working together to improve the teaching of writing in the nation's schools and in other settings. NWP provides high-quality professional development programs to teachers in a variety of disciplines and at all levels, from early childhood through university. Through its network of nearly 200 university-based sites, NWP develops the leadership, programs and research needed for teachers to help students become successful writers and learners.

Library of Congress Cataloging-in-Publication Data

Early, Jessica Singer.
Real world writing for secondary students : teaching the college admission essay and other gate-openers for higher education / Jessica Singer Early, Meredith DeCosta ; foreword by Charles Bazerman.
p. cm.— (Language and literacy series)
Includes bibliographical references.
ISBN 978-0-8077-5386-6 (pbk.)—ISBN 978-0-8077-5387-3 (hardcover)
1. English language—Composition and exercises—Study and teaching (Secondary)—United States. 2. College applications—United States. I. DeCosta, Meredith. II. Title.
LB1631.E27 2012
428.0071'2—dc23 2012028496

ISBN 978-0-8077-5386-6 (paperback)
ISBN 978-0-8077-5387-3 (hardcover)

Printed on acid-free paper

Manufactured in the United States of America

19 18 17 16 15 14 13 12 8 7 6 5 4 3 2 1

To Lucca, Jax, and Pippin
—JSE

To my family
—MRD

Contents

Foreword

In this important book Jessica Early and Meredith DeCosta describe a readily replicable set of activities that provide motivated, meaningful opportunities for writing development and helps potential first-generation higher education students gain university admission. The two author-researcher-teachers provide activities, lessons, and scaffolding (Chapter 4) for students in difficult circumstances. They diagnose and provide solutions for the tensions that impede students from developing strong statements (Chapter 5). Almost as a by-product of the learning experiences, the student writing provides poignant views into their lives, and their persistent strength in pursuing ambitions (Chapter 6).

We see the students at first anxious and uncertain about whether they belong in the university, whether they can be accepted, whether once accepted they will survive. Their first drafts are short and unelaborated, often far from the most important experiences of their lives. They represent themselves as they imagine a conventionally acceptable student might appear, although they themselves do not have much of the experiences of conventional students and have little knowledge of conventional students from which to create fictional conventional selves. The guidebook examples from more affluent and culturally dominant students the instructors initially offer are intimidating and not useful because the students at Libertad High School do not have the club participation, academic enrichment, and holiday travel that are the touchstones of conventionally successful application essays.

In the course of the workshop classes, however, the students learn to find their subjects in the events and motives that have shaped their lives and reveal their drive. They learn to elaborate on these events with the felt intensity of life. As writing teachers, the researchers are quick to realize that these tales from the student lives make for compelling reading and powerful essays likely to impress application readers. They abandon the conventional models and help students find models of personal narratives closer to their experience.

But there is something more here. Students have now been able to construct robust university-bound presences for themselves from which to interact and learn in their new environment. Rather than trying to pass as conventional students and continuing to wonder whether they belong, they will be aware they have been accepted at the university for who they are. They will address the excitement of the university fully fortified with all the motives, passions, and puzzles of their lives. Nontraditional students often have difficulty finding their way at the university and wind up being undistinguished students unless they can discover a workable identity that allows them to draw on their full beings as they address their academic challenges. Paradoxically, they often discover their most usable academic selves by drawing on their full identities that stretch far beyond the academy. The personally felt application essays the students from Libertad will have written allow them to walk in the door, already sure of who they are and ready to work.

The richer and more complete selves they are able to assert will transform their institutions as well. Universities are affected by who the students are and what they share with their peers and professors. Diverse students who confidently explore their interests and identities, rather than hiding behind uncertain conventionality, open up the experience of the university for all students and press the curriculum to address more needs and more viewpoints. As the Libertad students (and all the other students at their institutions) then make the next transition of their lives to the workplace and public sphere, they will bring with them an enriched set of experiences and engagements that come from robust diversity on campus.

A gateway not only is what one must pass through; it is a frame for announcing one's self to the world one is entering, the self that will engage in new experiences. What is true for universities and admissions essays is true for job applications and project proposals, for letters of introduction and personal websites, for all genres that present the self for new opportunities for interaction and growth. Our entry selves set in motion who we will become and, in becoming, transform those spaces for all others who share the space with us. Gates have two sides: from the front they are imposing; behind us, they mark starting points for new chapters in our lives.

—Charles Bazerman
Gevirtz Graduate School of Education,
University of California, Santa Barbara

Acknowledgments

Jessica would like to thank Charles Bazerman for his scholarship and teaching, which provided the foundation and inspiration for this book. Ruth Shagoury's encouragement was instrumental in the development of this project. Thank you to the students, teachers, and administrators who openly shared their writing, which is the heart of this study. Thank you to Meredith DeCosta, Arturo Valdespino, Cynthia Nicholson, and Sara Slagle, who each contributed their strengths as teachers and young scholars to the planning, teaching, coding, and writing found within these pages. Thank you to Meg Lemke for her support of this project in its early stages of development with Teachers College Press and to Emily Spangler for her support in the later stages. Thank you to Corinne Mooney at Teachers College Press for her careful reading and feedback. Thank you to Tom Newkirk, Sheridan Blau, and Kevin Roozen for their continuing encouragement. Thank you to the National Writing Project for their incredible network of support for the research and teaching of writing.

Jessica thanks her parents, George and Joanne Singer, who epitomize the meaning of sponsorship. Jessica's biggest debt is to her husband, Jake Early. Having a partner with humor, a sympathetic ear, and creative advice is invaluable, especially while raising three children under the age of 3 during the writing of this book.

Meredith would like to thank the writing teachers who have had a profound effect on her, including Duane Roen and Jean Wolph. She offers a special thanks to her mother, a middle school teacher, who taught her that teaching is not just a career; it's a way of being and moving through the world.

CHAPTER 1

Setting the Stage for a Study of Writing

Writing is one of humankind's most powerful tools. Its mastery is essential for success both in and out of school.

—Steve Graham & Karen Harris, 2005, p. 1

The study of writing described in this book was ignited years ago by the first author, Jessica, when she was teaching senior English in an urban high school in Portland, Oregon. She often lost sleep wondering and worrying about where students would end up after graduation and imagining ways she could rework curriculum to better support and prepare them for their next life steps. Through her teaching, Jessica witnessed ethnically and linguistically diverse students who had the grades, writing and reading abilities, and aspirations to attend 4-year universities and colleges but for various reasons graduated high school without post-secondary plans in place. She noticed that the majority of students who applied and were accepted to 4-year colleges and universities, internships, and jobs had been in Honors or Advanced Placement classes and were middle- or upper-class and White. Conversely, most students in non–college prep or regular English classes did not have clear post-secondary plans and were low-income students of color.

She addressed this inequity by embedding real world writing genres into her secondary English curriculum to demystify the kinds of writing tasks required for post-secondary schooling and programs such as Teach for America or AmeriCorps (see Singer, 2006, 2007; Singer & Hubbard, 2003). She chose to focus more of her curriculum on the teaching of writing instead of just reading. She designed and implemented real world reading and writing tasks, including conducting interviews, participating in public speaking activities, and preparing resumes and cover letters for work and internship opportunities. She gave students opportunities to write for real audiences and for real purposes to help them plan and prepare for life after high school. Through this work, Jessica experienced firsthand how writing can open doors for students. Without practice, feedback, and support, she realized her students would be left on their own to figure out complicated and consequential writing genres that could make a difference in their future lives.

First as a high school English teacher, and now years later as researcher and teacher educator, Jessica is committed to securing literacy opportunities for youth that will benefit them in college and beyond. She is interested in examining ways secondary English language arts teachers may embed real world and gate-opening writing genres, like the college admission essay, into the curriculum to better serve the needs of all students.

An important motivation for undertaking the research and teaching described in this book is the long-standing American belief that "successful people pull themselves up by their bootstraps"; this is simply not the case. Successful individuals in our society and, more specifically, in our school system, usually have access to and receive academic support. The path Jessica took to arrive in her current position as a university professor and to gain the required skill set for this work helps to prove this point. Her path was paved with important figures of support, starting with family members and extending to teachers, family friends, and community mentors. Jessica comes from a family of educators who continually exposed her to reading and writing activities at home and provided ongoing support with homework and gate-opening writing tasks that are prized in institutions of power. Because of this support, she moved through the education system with relative ease. She now turns this support outward to try to understand how she, and the education system we are all a part of, can provide better access to literacy for all students, especially those whose paths to success are more challenging than her own.

RESEARCH QUESTIONS

This book describes a case study Jessica implemented, with help from her research assistants and the classroom teachers, of a gate-opening writing workshop for ethnically and linguistically diverse high school students. Students who took part in this workshop received instruction on specific genre features of college admission essays. This is a study of curricular and teaching choices as well as an examination of student response to a real world and gate-opening writing curriculum. The following research questions guide this work:

a. What curricular and teaching choices take place in the design and implementation of a 6-week writing workshop for ethnically and linguistically diverse secondary students using explicit teaching of college admission essay genre features?

b. What stories do ethnically and linguistically diverse secondary students share when provided the opportunity to write college admission essays within the formal English language arts curriculum?

c. What rewards and obstacles do secondary English language arts teachers, researchers, and students face when taking part in a real world, gate-opening writing curriculum?

This book attempts to illuminate the many layers that go into creating, teaching, and researching the writing practices of ethnically and linguistically diverse secondary students.

STUDYING ACROSS BOUNDARIES

Jessica has shared initial findings from this study along with her research team at a number of national conferences and professional workshops where she has received useful feedback, suggestions, and support from colleagues. However, she has also received comments regarding the fact that she is a White, middle-class woman studying ethnically and linguistically diverse students and how this may in some ways diminish or complicate the findings or inhibit her perspective as a researcher. There are no easy answers for these comments. Jessica wants to acknowledge the ways her race, gender, and socioeconomic background impact her research lens. However, she takes the position that it is possible for researchers to study across boundaries of race and social class. Because she has received the gifts of sponsorship and access to education and institutions of power, she want to pass those gifts along to her graduate students, teachers, secondary students, and schools. It is her hope that by researching about issues of access and equity connected to secondary literacy practices and then sharing what she learns with a broad audience through writing, she can work toward positive social change.

THE POWER OF LANGUAGE: DEFINING KEY TERMS

Too often, language choices in studies involving ethnically and linguistically diverse students are inconsistent or made without careful consideration. Researchers and theorists are engaged in ongoing debates about the ways language can unfairly categorize, label, dehumanize, or devalue individuals (Kinloch, 2010a; Paris, 2011a). The terms utilized in this text were selected to help fairly portray the research and teaching team, the study participants, and the rationale and beliefs behind this work. Many of the terms are commonly and sensibly used in the realm of writing research and literacy studies.

Terms of Collaboration

The research and teaching process are neither solo nor simple acts. This project is a collaborative effort that took place over 5 years. Jessica began by drawing together a research and teaching team to assist with the curricular design of the college admission essay workshop, teaching, data collection and analysis, and write-up of this work. In the pages that follow, "we" is used to describe Jessica along with the second author, Meredith, who contributed to the following pages through her assistance researching the college admission essay genre, conducting data analysis, and writing up findings. The term *research and teaching team* (described in detail in Chapter 3) is used to describe the entire team of teachers and researchers involved in the study, including Jessica and Meredith; the two classroom teachers, Sarah and Dan; and the graduate and undergraduate research assistants, Arturo, Cynthia, and Sara.

Demographic Terms

The term *English language learner (ELL)* describes students who first learned a language other than English in their home or community and then, at a later time, learned English as a new language. *Ethnically and linguistically diverse* describes the population of the school and the student makeup of the two classrooms where this study took place. These terms refer to students who come from non-dominant racial, cultural, ethnic, and linguistic groups. *Latino* describes students and parents in this study who were first- or second-generation Mexican Americans, meaning their parents were originally from Mexico. Although some students in this study are Mexican American, Hispanic, Latino/a, and/or Chicano/a, the term *Latino* is used to describe this population collectively and for consistency. The term *low-income* describes economically underprivileged communities with limited access to financial wealth. Many, although not all, of the students who come from low-income communities take part in the free and reduced lunch school program. The phrase *underserved students* is used to describe students who are too often forgotten or left behind by the school system. There are persistent inequalities in the access certain populations have to material resources, time, and attention from teachers, administrators, and policymakers. These students are often second language learners, students of color, and students who come from low-income neighborhoods. The words *underserved school settings* depict the kinds of schools in our country that have historically been under-resourced and forced to operate without sufficient economic or social support.

Sponsorship

This book borrows from and expands upon Brandt's (2001) definition and frame of writing sponsorship. In *Literacy in American Lives* (2001), Brandt describes the multiplicity of influences on individuals' writing practices, what she calls *sponsors*, which both limit and facilitate literacy development. She defines sponsors as "any agents, local or distant, concrete or abstract, who enable, support, teach, and model, as well as recruit, regulate, suppress, or withhold literacy—and gain advantage by it in some way" (p. 19). Brandt's study is based on 80 1- to 3-hour interviews "with a diverse group of Americans ranging in birth date from the late 1890s to the early 1980s" (p. 9). Brandt examines sponsorship outside the immediate school and classroom context, and instead points to large-scale economic and social influences on the acquisition of literacy. "No teacher or policy maker at any level can ignore the power of the country's economic system, its direction of change in the twentieth century, and the implications that brings, especially now, for literacy, and literacy learning" (p. 43). She also considers regional, cultural, and family influences on the development of writing abilities and how these influences reflect larger changes in American life. Brandt's (2001) well-established approach to studying individuals' lifetime literacy practices through sponsorship offers a promising way to contribute to writing research.

Rather than examining writing development from a social and economic perspective using a macro lens, the following pages examine writing from a case study perspective within a classroom context. This work is primarily interested in understanding the ways English language arts teachers serve to facilitate literacy learning and how they may act as important and necessary writing sponsors for their students by embedding real world and gate-opening writing into their curriculum.

Gatekeeping Writing

One of the ways secondary students succeed in the everyday written work of school is by mastering specific genre forms, and more specifically, by mastering real world, gatekeeping genres that work to advance their educational and occupational pursuits. The term *gatekeeping writing* is used to describe those genres of writing that hold power in institutions of power such as schools and businesses. These are the writing tasks that can, in part, open or close the doors of opportunity to students depending on whether students complete them successfully and whether students follow the expectations of the community that constructs or mediates the task.

The term *gate-opening writing* is frequently used in lieu of *gatekeeping writing*. This term is synonymous with gatekeeping writing; however, it is used to emphasize the importance of believing in what is possible when students learn real world genres of writing, rather than seeing these writing tasks as rigid, indestructible barriers that students cannot learn or overcome.

On a broader scale, the phrase *gate-opening* is emblematic of the possibilities of education despite distinct barriers for many students. Historically, politically, and educationally, many youth have missed opportunities to succeed in institutions of power because of their racial, ethnic, socioeconomic, or cultural identities. This book does not intend to diminish these issues or deny that they exist. Instead, it offers a vision of what is possible despite these challenges, especially with the collective effort of students and teachers. Consider the marginalized students who break down these barriers by seeking out the support and resources to achieve success in institutions of power. Now consider the teachers who are committed to opening the gates for students by providing them with literacy skills and strategies necessary to open doors to their future lives. This is what it means when students and their teachers "open the gates."

Real world Writing

Real world writing describes writing tasks where students identify a real audience beyond the classroom teacher, have empathy and understanding for that audience, and attempt to reach that audience through appropriate content, purpose, and conventions (Gallagher, 2011; Wiggins, 2009). "Real world" and "gate-opening" writing help explain and differentiate the kinds of writing that should be embedded more often in secondary language arts curriculum, particularly in classrooms made up of ethnically and linguistically diverse students. Even though real world writing comes in many different genres, addresses a variety of audiences, and serves a number of purposes, it is essential for communicating well, obtaining a job, and advancing a career. Real world writing requires that a writer meet the specific needs of an actual audience within a rhetorical context and engage that audience in the topic.

Real world writing can also be defined by what it is not. It is not a prompt designed to test reading comprehension or to measure writing correctness with no audience other than the classroom teacher in mind (Wiggins, 2009)—for example, an assignment designed to prove whether a student completed the required reading for a homework assignment. Examples of real world, gate-opening genres include college admission essays, resumes, aptitude and scholarship essays, interviews, technical reports and brochures, community newsletters, letters to the editor, and various forms of multimodal digital writing, such as blogs (Cope & Kalantizis, 1993, 2000; Donovan & Smolkin, 2006; Lankshear & Knobel, 2003; Martin, 1989). These are real world genres because they require writers to have a real audience, to have an understanding of the needs of that audience, and to meet the audience's needs through the use of a variety of genre conventions. For example, when students participate in writing cover letters for summer internship programs at local businesses, camps, and community organizations, they engage with a real audience and their writing has real consequences attached. The cover letters for this particular purpose are formal and professional in tone and carry certain expectations. For example, the writer is expected to demonstrate an understanding and vested interest in the program as well as his or her interest, expertise, and motivation for pursuing the internship.

Real world writing, like the internship cover letter, elicits a reaction or feedback from an audience, which can result in an invitation, an acceptance or rejection, a request, additional attention, or an offer of some kind. For example, when students write, revise, and submit letters to the editor of a local newspaper based on a topic they are invested in and have researched thoroughly, they become engaged in a real world conversation or dialogue with the editor and with the ideas presented in the news. The audience is not confined to the classroom and is not imagined, but becomes a professional with the power to respond, react to, publish, or ignore the students' written work. In short, there are powerful consequences for the success or failure of a piece of writing, and teachers are in a unique position to show real world writing and its consequences to students.

Social Justice

The terms *social justice* and *teaching for social justice* are used throughout this text. These terms are foundational to the study and an essential part of what should be the purpose of education (Singer, 2006). This research stems from a long line of literacy educators—like Paulo Freire, Sonia Nieto, Anne Haas Dyson, Linda Darling-Hammond, JoBeth Allen, Randy Bomer, Carole Edelsky, and Linda Christensen—who have brought issues of equity and justice to the forefront of their work in literacy classrooms. The term *social justice* is used in three ways:

a. To suggest that educators must push back against the power structures that inhibit students' intellectual, emotional, and physical freedoms
b. To highlight the notion that social consciousness and individual liberation can flourish when youth are encouraged to recognize and use these power structures to better their lives and become contributing members of a democratic society
c. To emphasize how writing is a transformative and political act that can help open doors for students and position them for success in the academy, the workplace, and the community.

A PLACE FOR REAL WORLD WRITING IN THE CURRICULUM

The description and findings of this study of college admission essay writing are not meant to give the impression that learning about the college admission essay, or any other specific writing task, can or should replace rich curriculum that encourages students to engage in critical thinking and writing. Teachers should avoid teaching real world writing tasks as decontextualized recipes or forms but, instead, as part of larger discussions, projects, and units that provide students with access to critical thinking (Singer, 2006). One way to avoid this decontextualization is to embed real world writing tasks into ongoing curricular units of inquiry. Teachers may provide students with the opportunity to engage in fruitful discussions about why certain writing forms, such as the college admission essay and high-stakes testing on-demand essays, are deemed more critical than others and who decides that certain tasks hold more weight in institutions of power than, say, a short story, poem, or play. Students may explore how writing functions as a source of cultural capital that they can harness and use to their benefit. Teaching tasks like the college admission essay can also open opportunities for teachers to talk about audience, including knowing who you are writing for and why, as well as the importance of both speaking to and pushing back against genres of writing that hold power in college and beyond.

As more colleges place emphasis on the college admission essay and other forms of writing as key criteria to determine admission, conversation at post-secondary institutions about what makes a successful college admission essay should also increase. Transparency and openness from post-secondary institutions regarding the admission process should be improved. After an exhaustive phone and Internet search to find information provided by colleges, universities, or the College Board about the specific audience for college admission essays, we found nothing concrete. We could not find a common rubric or list of criteria that colleges or universities use to assess the quality of admission essays. This is disconcerting. Resources to help students demystify the college admission process should be more readily available, and this is necessary if institutions of higher education are serious about attracting, recruiting, and admitting first-generation college students and students from ethnically, linguistically, culturally, and economically diverse backgrounds.

INVITATION TO READERS

This book is for pre- and in-service teachers, literacy coaches, school leaders, researchers, and all those involved in English language arts education who want to see a greater emphasis on the teaching of writing in classrooms and who want to address the imbalances in writing instruction at the secondary level. It is also for educators who want to promote democracy and justice in U.S. schools. The curriculum, teachers, and students described in this book offer some of the many avenues educators can take to shift the imbalances in both education and social systems. Educators must continue to turn their attention to the literacy needs of ethnically and linguistically diverse students, the forces that impact their learning, the types of literacies currently taking place in secondary English classrooms, and the demands of changing literacies on society and schooling. By examining and addressing these different aspects of literacy through pedagogical and curricular development and research, they can start to meet the needs of an increasingly diverse student population. This book hopes to engage educators and researchers in a conversation about the importance of real world writing and its potential impact on secondary students as they move toward college and beyond.

The case study described in this book is intended to support educators who may try to implement a similar curriculum, as well as those literacy researchers who feel compelled to address the needs of low-income, ethnically and linguistically diverse writers in secondary classrooms and can see the usefulness of this kind of research. This study offers insight into two classrooms and one writing curriculum, illustrating how change is possible through creative pedagogy and curriculum and devoted teachers.

Above all, this book is a call to experienced educators to renew the need for social justice and equity in schools. It is an invitation to secondary teachers—faced with pressure to demonstrate student success on high-stakes tests and to follow state and national policy mandates—to think of writing as a vital tool for all students to succeed academically and professionally. These pages work to re-conceptualize the ways in which writing can best serve ethnically and linguistically diverse students and best address the persistent inequities in schools. Novice and expert teachers are encouraged to breathe life into their work by infusing instructional practices with pedagogy and curriculum that matters beyond their classroom walls—the kind that opens gates for all students to succeed.

OVERVIEW OF THE BOOK

Chapter 2 describes an overview of current research and work devoted to the teaching of writing in secondary schools, especially schools in ethnically and linguistically diverse communities. This chapter also describes the theoretical framework, drawing connections between cultural capital and genre theory and illustrating how genre can function as both form and social action.

Chapter 3 describes the school and classroom context for this study as well as the students, classroom teachers, and research and teaching team who worked together to make this project possible.

Chapter 4 focuses on a case study of one real world, gate-opening writing workshop on college admission essays and offers a discussion of the importance of the college admission essay genre, an overview of the writing workshop, and the key genre elements and skill lessons students engaged in during the workshop. (The term *skill lesson* is used instead of *mini-lesson* to avoid suggesting that these complex, time-consuming lessons are diminutive.) The chapter showcases students' writing and the impact of the workshop on the quality of students' college admission essays.

Chapter 5 dives more deeply into the analysis of the college admission essays and highlights the points of tension and obstacles that the research and teaching team and students faced during and after the workshop, as well as the opportunities that can emerge from such analysis. We also explore self-efficacy and reflection, as well as the role they played, in this writing workshop. We conclude the chapter by sharing lingering questions about ways this workshop could be extended and improved upon.

Chapter 6 explores the deeply personal, self-revelatory essays students wrote regarding challenging lived experiences as well as their dexterity negotiating multiple cultural, ethnic, and linguistic identities. We demonstrate the value of what ethnically and linguistically diverse writers bring to educational institutions through college admission essays, regardless of whether their stories and lived experiences have traditionally been deemed significant for this genre. We argue for secondary writing curriculum, as well as college admission panels, to honor the voices of ethnically and linguistically diverse secondary writers and to advocate for the acceptance and inclusion of real world, gate-opening writing tasks that enhance students' writing capital in the secondary classroom.

Chapter 7 explores the different stakeholders involved in the schooling process and how they may help create a culture of real world, gate-opening writing in secondary schools. We also offer insight into the research and teaching process described in Chapters 1–6 and discuss the implications for this kind of work on researchers, teachers, and students. The book concludes with a call to all those vested in writing at the secondary level to view real world, gate-opening writing as an integral means to addressing the inequities that continue to face our nation's schools.

CHAPTER 2

Why Writing Matters

Writing today is not a frill for the few, but an essential skill for the many.

—National Commission on Writing for America's Schools and Colleges, 2003, p. 11

The past 25 years have brought about significant changes in the ways writing is constructed, shared, taught, and assessed. Many of these developments have taken place as part of the onset of advanced technologies, increased access to the Internet and digital forms of literacy, and the economic and social demands of globalization. These changes have led the National Council of Teachers of English (NCTE) and other important literacy organizations to issue statements on the complexities and intricacies of 21st-century writing (NCTE, 2008). The 2001 No Child Left Behind Act (NCLB) also has had a significant impact on writing instruction, shifting schools' focus away from 21st-century writing and toward an emphasis on the teaching and assessing of reading (Applebee & Langer, 2009). Despite these changes, the literacy practice least likely to be found in most English language arts classrooms is writing, even though students must acquire proficient and versatile writing skills to succeed in school and gain access to college and the workplace (Brandt, 2001; Hull & Schultz, 2002).

In recent years, a number of studies and commissions have explored the range of writing practices taking place in schools. Across the board, these studies have shown that alarmingly high numbers of secondary students are not meeting basic levels of writing proficiency. Further, ethnically and linguistically diverse students at the secondary and college levels are falling behind their White peers in writing achievement (National Assessment of Educational Progress [NAEP], 2009).

THE NEGLECTED "R"

In July 2003, the U.S. Department of Education released *The Nation's Report Card Writing 2002*, a report outlining results from the NAEP 2002 writing assessment at grades 4, 8, and 12, which was the most comprehensive assessment of writing ever conducted in the United States. The results reveal that fewer than one in three 4th-graders, one in three 8th-graders, and one in four 12th-graders scored at or above the proficient level in writing. They also reveal significant gaps in performance between ethnically and linguistically diverse students and their White counterparts. The 2003 report (U.S. Department of Education, 2003) also showed that although there had been an increase in classroom writing throughout the United States between 1988 and 1998, the majority of students were not taking part in complex, lengthy, or real world writing assignments. This is of significant concern for secondary students hoping to pursue higher education or enter the workforce, where the demands for writing are complex and multifaceted (American Diploma Project, 2004).

Equally disconcerting are the recent reports of the types of school writing 8th-grade students participated in between 2002 and 2007. The results show a significant drop in the practice of every form of writing students were asked about, including interpretation and analysis, persuasive letters and essays, personal and imaginative stories and observations, and professional writing (Applebee & Langer, 2009; NAEP, 2007). Moreover, a study by ACT (2005) shows that close to one-third of high school students planning to attend post-secondary institutions do not meet readiness benchmarks for college composition courses and 50% or more of adolescents in certain ethnic groups do not meet ACT benchmarks, placing them at a great disadvantage in their transition to and overall success in college.

Furthermore, in May 2006, the National Commission on Writing in America's Schools and Colleges (2006) released the report *Writing and School Reform including the Neglected "R": The Need for a Writing Revolution*. This landmark report called for a significant increase in the time, resources, and technologies devoted to writing instruction and practice in K–12 schools. To address the problem of the neglected "R," in 2004, the National Commission on Writing and its advisory panel held five meetings, or seminars, in five locations throughout the United States to engage in discussions and elicit feedback. During these seminars, classroom teachers, principals, curriculum coordinators, university administrators, researchers, and policymakers met to discuss what counts as effective writing instruction and how to better meet the needs of all students. The commission (2006) concluded that educators must:

a. personalize writing instruction
b. create a sense of community around writing and writers
c. make writing a part of policy reformd. improve professional development.

The commission also found that models of effective writing instruction require students to be active participants in the learning process, and that educators must encourage students to write for public audiences; call on students to collect, analyze, and synthesize sources; and invite students to use their home culture and language as a resource.

IMPROVING WRITING AND WRITING INSTRUCTION

With these challenges and goals in mind, educators and policymakers across the United States have set out to improve writing instruction, including instruction at the secondary level. The National Writing Project (NWP), National Council of Teachers of English (NCTE), Conference on College Composition and Communication (CCCC), and Council of Writing Program Administrators (CWPA) are just some organizations that have begun to extend their networks, growing their membership and outreach and using online resources to improve writing instruction across grade levels. For example, the NWP continued to expand its professional development and leadership opportunities for K–college teachers of writing. The organization now has more than 200 university-based writing project sites, which span all 50 states, Washington, D.C., Puerto Rico, and the Virgin Islands. The National Writing Project is also collaborating with the Center on English Learning and Achievement to conduct a new national study on writing instruction across grades and subjects.

Many groups also have come together to address the issue of college readiness, recognizing that writing is key to students' success in college and the workplace. The best-known example is the *Framework for Success in Postsecondary Writing* (2011), which was developed by the CWPA, NCTE, and NWP. Based on current writing pedagogy research, the framework offers a series of mental habits and rhetorical and 21st-century skills that students need to succeed in college and college writing. One of the primary goals of the framework is to help teachers develop sound habits and skills with students through writing, reading, and critical analysis. As organizations and commissions have ramped up their efforts to improve student writing and writing instruction, there has also been a greater focus on research designed to examine the writing practices of ethnically and linguistically diverse students in academic contexts from kindergarten to graduate school, as well as out-of-school contexts like the workplace and community (Ball, 2006; Beaufort, 1999; Edelsky, 1986; Faltis & Wolfe, 1999; Guerra, 1998; Hull & Schultz, 2002; Valdes, 2001). A number of studies in ethnically and linguistically diverse school communities have focused on the impact of specific instructional strategies on students' writing development. For example, researchers have examined the impact of

a. teaching argument (Yeh & Smart, 1998)
b. extending classroom writing opportunities (Davis, Clarke, & Rhodes, 1994)
c. using writing to make connections between lived experience and poetry (Agee, 1995)
d. teaching analytical writing (Carbonaro & Gamoran, 2002)
e. using writing in connection to book clubs (Kong & Fitch, 2002/2003)
f. incorporating self-sponsored and familial-based writing practices into writing curriculum (Brandt, 2001; Early, 2010; Heath, 1983).

There also have been a number of recent studies of youth language and literacy practices in multilingual and multiethnic schools and communities (Fisher, 2007; Kirkland, 2010; Paris, 2010, 2011b; Winn, 2011). These studies illuminate the language and literacy practices of ethnically and linguistically diverse youth in both academic and out-of-school contexts. Despite greater focus on the literacy practices of diverse learners in and out of school, there is still little information about teaching writing to ethnically and linguistically diverse students at the secondary level (Ball, 2006).

To confirm the need for further research in this area, ethnically and linguistically diverse learners who attend schools in low-income and under-resourced communities are not acquiring the writing skills needed to succeed in today's competitive and technologically advanced society (Ball, 2006). Many ethnically and linguistically diverse secondary students in the United States do not obtain the basic writing skills necessary to pass state-mandated high school competency exams, and few ethnically and linguistically diverse secondary students enroll in the college preparatory English courses required to gain admission to college and universities (NCES, 2007; Ruiz-de-Velasco & Fix, 2000). This book adds to the growing and much-needed discussion on effective ways of teaching writing by focusing on the value of teaching real world and gate-opening writing tasks to prepare students for their transition to college, the workplace, and life beyond high school.

WRITING AS CULTURAL CURRENCY

To contextualize our argument regarding the power of real world and gate-opening writing and the importance of embedding this kind of writing into the secondary English language arts curriculum, we outline two intersecting theories that frame much of this text: cultural capital and genre theory.

Cultural Capital

Cultural capital can be defined as the non-economic skills, abilities, and goods that help promote a person's social mobility. This concept primarily derives from the work of sociologist Pierre Bourdieu (1979/1984), who argues that individuals acquire cultural capital through familial practices and formal schooling. He suggests that the skills, abilities, or goods individuals acquire in their home lives and through formal schooling help determine their status in society. For example, middle- and upper-class children may have access to computers and other forms of computer technology such as iPads and Kindles in their homes. Exposure to these highly prized literacy forms often helps place these children at an advantage by the time they enter school.

Although much research on cultural capital has been devoted to the consumption of and participation in highbrow culture, such as art and theater (Lareau, 2006; Lareau & Weininger, 2003), this book focuses on the cultural strategies that individuals and groups use to gain access to institutions of power like schools (Bourdieu, 1979/1984; Bourdieu & Passeron, 1977).

Gaining Access to School. U.S. schools prize certain forms of the English language and Standard English is one form that schools commonly accept and acknowledge over all other forms. Oral and written fluency in Standard English often helps students access Advanced Placement or higher-level college preparatory courses and curriculum as well as pass language-based achievement tests (Gandara & Rumberger, 2009). This means that the academic achievement, ability levels, and language competencies of youth are social and political constructs rather than signs of innate intelligence or giftedness (Ball, 2000; Fisher, 2007; Kinloch, 2010b). The cultural capital youth possess directly impacts their position in society, particularly in school settings. Studies show that students who possess certain forms of cultural capital—for example, those who come from economic wealth and come from high-status families—earn better grades in high school (DiMaggio, 1982) and attend more selective colleges and universities (Jordan, 2010) than students who do not have particular types of cultural capital. These same studies also claim that teachers favor students who possess certain kinds of cultural capital by rewarding them with more attention and by lauding their efforts and work.

Other research extends the definition of cultural capital by suggesting that cultural capital also refers to which academic skills students gain access to and what academic skills are privileged by institutions of power (Lareau & Weininger, 2003). For example, Lareau and Weininger conducted an ethnographic study demonstrating how a middle-class African American family exhibited cultural capital in a way that an African American family below the poverty line did not. In this study, the middle-class parents were more apt to supervise, monitor, and intervene with teachers and school administrators regarding their child's academics. For example, the mother described in the study used her informal networks to have her daughter re-tested through a private agency to get into a gifted and talented program even though the daughter had scored too poorly on the test to meet the requirement the first time. The mother's involvement and persistence paid off and her daughter was accepted into the accelerated program. The mother knew how to communicate and work with and around the school system to promote her daughter's access to an accelerated academic program. The study also demonstrates how exposure to this kind of parental involvement and intervention also rubbed off on the children. Through this informal modeling, the children learned how to imitate and incorporate this behavior into their own academic lives to their advantage. In contrast, the family in the study that lived below the poverty line was not familiar with educational jargon often used by school community members and was less communicative with teachers and administrators. As a result, they were less inclined to speak to school authorities or advocate on their child's behalf. Therefore, the children were not positioned the same way as the children from the middle-class family. Studies like this suggest that cultural capital—namely the skills, abilities, and goods students are exposed to, surrounded by, and expected to possess—influences students' position and experiences in school and their access to institutions beyond the classroom.

This book focuses on the kinds of literacy capital students need to gain access to college, the workplace, and beyond, and to be successful in institutions of power. Although there are many forms of literacy capital, including linguistic and literary, this study is focused on writing capital.

Writing Capital. Writing capital is acquired through practicing the specific writing skills and forms that individuals need to function effectively, efficiently, and successfully in institutions of power. Drawing from Bourdieu's work, Compton-Lilly (2009) cites three kinds of writing capital: economic, social, and cultural. Economic writing capital includes tangible possessions, such as laptops and iPads, that students use to support writing. Social writing capital includes the relationships students form with teachers and peers to support their development as writers. Cultural writing capital involves "culturally valued ways of being, knowing, and acting relative to writing" (Compton-Lilly, p. 6). This includes the building and procuring of writing skills, products, and accolades to demonstrate writing proficiency, like passing standardized writing tests. Writing capital is a powerful tool that students can accumulate and use over a lifetime. If students are exposed to writing capital in various formats for an extended period, they can then begin to make these strategies and tactics part of their own habits, perceptions, and attitudes (Compton-Lilly, 2009).

In our advocacy of writing capital in classrooms, we do not want to suggest that students who have not been exposed to the cultural capital of institutions of power are culturally deficient. Bourdieu (1979/1984) critiques this notion, but many researchers and teachers have misinterpreted or misused the theory of cultural capital to argue that students from low-income, ethnically and linguistically diverse communities are in some way lacking or devoid of culture (García & Guerra, 2004; Yosso, 2005). This simply is not the case. Educators should value the "aspirational, navigational, social, linguistic, familial and resistant capital" (Yosso, p. 69) that students from underserved communities bring to the classroom. Researchers and educators can break down barriers between home and school by drawing from students' experiences to navigate through mandated curricula (Morrell & Duncan-Andrade, 2002; Street, 2005). Writing researchers and educators can work to create more equitable learning experiences by valuing the cultural practices students bring to the classroom from their home lives and communities while demystifying writing genres that carry significant weight in academic, professional, and civic contexts.

Genre Theory

Complementing Bourdieu's (1979/1984) theory of cultural capital is genre theory, which considers writing to be a form of social action (Cope & Kalantizis, 1993; Dean, 2008; Donovan & Smolkin, 2006; Martin, 1989; Purcell-Gates, Duke, & Martineau, 2007). Enacting certain genres through writing allows individuals to become social actors with capital and power. Through genre, writers learn "not just a pattern of forms or even a method of achieving our own ends. We learn, more importantly, what ends we might have" (Miller, 1984, p. 165). Over the past 30 years, thinking about genre has shifted from simply understanding texts as templates or categorizing texts based on form—like deciding a poem should be called a poem because it has particular conventions such as rhythm and meter—to considering the ways texts are a direct reflection of and deeply tied to social norms and expectations. The five-paragraph essay is an example of genre form that is deeply rooted in K–12 teaching practices and expectations. This form requires the writer to organize his or her thoughts using an introduction, three body paragraphs, and a conclusion.

Although most writing that takes place in colleges and universities, the workplace, and the community does not fit into a five-paragraph format, this has become one of the most widely taught curricular tools for K–12 teachers of writing across grade levels. At its best, it is meant to serve simply as a foundational structure to help beginning writers; at its worst, it is the only form students are exposed to as they progress in school. Regardless, it is one of the most commonly accepted and expected writing forms for students to master prior to college (Johnson, Thompson, Smagorinsky, & Fry, 2003).

Bazerman and Prior (2005) argue that genre theory has three different perspectives: genre as text, genre as rhetoric, and genre as practice. The *genre as text* perspective focuses on genre conventions as reflections of a particular social situation. Writing forms are fluid and flexible, continually shifting to fit the values and contexts of a social group. *Genre as rhetoric* emphasizes the social situations that surround various textual forms. The third perspective, *genre as practice,* begins with the contexts and processes of genre rather than the genre form itself. For example, Spinuzzi (2003) examined the ways many workplace genres are designed to support employees in their thinking and in taking action rather than just being a way for employees to communicate internally or externally.

Miller's influential 1984 article "Genre as Social Action" helped set the stage for thinking about genres as performing important social functions. From this perspective, writers create texts that are always acknowledging and acting in meaningful ways within social contexts. These social contexts set, maintain, and shift expectations for the way language is used. From these expectations a genre or set of genres emerges (Bazerman, 1997; Prior, 2006; Purcell-Gates et al., 2007; Swales, 1990). Bazerman (2004) asserts, "Each successful text creates for its readers a social fact," and, in turn, "becomes part of the way humans give shape to social activity" (pp. 311 & 317).

Yet discourse and research on writing and genre primarily exist at the college (Charney & Carlson, 1995; Yancey, 2000) and elementary levels (Cheng, 2008; Hyland, 2007; Ramanathan & Kaplan, 2000), with a gap in between. Researchers have yet to widely apply these perspectives on writing at the secondary level, and there are few empirical studies of instructional practices designed to support genre knowledge with secondary students (Donovan & Smolkin, 2006; Graham & Perin, 2007a; Hillocks, 1986).

Explicit Teaching of Genre. It is easy for English educators to focus instruction on understanding content and then leave students on their own to figure out how these gate-opening writing tasks actually function.

Sometimes, educators expect students to just know how to write an essay or a review without actually teaching them what these genres look like, how they function, for whom they are written, and how best to meet the audience's needs. However, the more experience students have with various real world writing tasks, the more they learn to comfortably navigate diverse forms of writing in different and important social contexts. By extension, students who are exposed to a variety of genres of writing at home or in their extracurricular and academic support programs become familiar with the genre expectations and are often placed at an advantage over students who are not exposed to or do not have access to these writing tasks. This suggests the importance of including real world, gate-opening genres in the secondary language arts curriculum and teaching all students how these written tasks function in both form and action, especially ethnically and linguistically diverse youth who frequently miss out on these tasks in school (Christensen, 2000, 2009; Kinloch, 2008; Kohn, 1999; Morrell, 2007; Nieto, 2009).

A number of studies examine the impact of explicit teaching of genre features on elementary children's writing (Kamberelis, 1999; Purcell-Gates et al., 2007). These studies focus on the explicit teaching of text structure, specifically text structure of story, exposition, and poetry. The results of these studies show that the explicit teaching of text structures improves children's understanding of and ability to write in those genres (Englert, Stewart, & Hiebert, 1988; Fitzgerald & Teasley, 1986; Schnoor, 2004). In another study, Purcell-Gates and colleagues (2007) found a strong relationship between the authenticity of reading and writing activities connected to texts and growth in students' abilities related to the genre. When students engaged with authentic genres, they were more likely to understand how the genre functions. This work suggests the importance of involving students in writing with real-life purposes. When educators expose students to a particular genre and give them the chance to learn how that genre operates, they increase students' knowledge and command of that genre (Duke, 2000; Purcell-Gates, 1996; Taylor & Dorsey-Gaines, 1988).

Skeptics about the nature of teaching genres also exist. Miller (1984), for example, cautions against teaching the features of genres as an overly simplified set of rules that are removed from the communities in which a genre is used. Scholars have expressed concerns that genre conventions can become stagnant and devoid of context and meaning if a writer is not aware of his or her context, goals, and intentions (Smagorinsky, Daigle, O'Donnell-Allen, & Bynum, 2010). Although writing should not be prescriptive or solely focused on form, understanding genres, how genres function, and the various rules and expectations associated with different kinds of writing is an important step toward academic success. In their 2010 study on academic writing, Smagorinsky, Daigle, O'Donnell-Allen, and Bynum found that even when a writer does not possess sufficient content knowledge, he or she may employ enough knowledge of the written genre and its conventions to create the impression that he or she has knowledge of the content.

Genres of Power. Although genres are always evolving (Freedman, 1993; Miller, 1984), as Smagorinsky et al. (2010) suggest, certain genres of writing hold power and affect students' academic success and their everyday lives at the high school and college level. For instance, over 60% of writing tasks at the undergraduate and graduate level are academic essays (Moore & Morton, 1999). The academic essay appears frequently in high schools, colleges, and universities and is an important part of what it means to "do school" (Cope & Kalantizis, 1993; Martin, 1989; Pope, 2001). Other types of writing, such as summaries, responses to texts, and collations of others' work, exemplify genres that are commonly found at the high school and college level and beyond. These genres hold significant social power in academic, professional, and civic settings. When students invoke a particular genre in their writing and use it successfully, they assert their identity as writers, learners, students, and individuals. Students should have access to a variety of genres, particularly genres of power, to gain access to the kinds of cultural capital necessary to be a part of whatever discourse community they choose.

Genre is becoming more and more essential, too, as 21st-century literacies have changed what, when, where, and why individuals write. As Prior (2006) notes, the "vast complexity of literate activity" (p. 63) in modern-day society requires that writers continually learn new genres and adapt their writing practices to new genres as they arise. For example, technology users are learning to read and enact genres such as computer-mediated visuals. Instead of fearing new genres or leaving genre forms out of the classroom entirely, educators may see these changes as a means of informing writing instruction at all levels, from kindergarten through college. Writing educators and researchers must be prepared to teach and explore genre with students, particularly those genres that influence the kinds of cultural capital students possess and those that hold weight in schools, the workplace, and beyond.

Keep in mind: We are not advocating that teachers solely teach the genres of power. Doing so may result in reproducing power structures rather than breaking them down. But, as Delpit (1995) argues, "Students must be taught the codes needed to participate fully in the mainstream of American life" (p. 45). Students deserve access to powerful forms of cultural capital, including the kinds of writing found at universities, the workplace, and our local communities. Some students may ultimately decide not to participate in institutions of power and may want to carve out their own literacy practices and habits (Cintron, 1998; Paris, 2010), which is fair. However, as Delpit contends, the opportunity for access should be available to all students, regardless of their ethnic or linguistic background.

One way to provide students with opportunities to learn dominant and gate-opening forms of cultural capital is to teach written genres that matter in the real world (Purcell-Gates et al., 2007). If secondary teachers expose all students to these genres, this may increase students' cultural capital and their ability to use it in their young adult lives.

CHAPTER 3

Constructing Our Case Study

> *Any educational setting—a classroom, a school, a family, a community program—is overflowing with human experiences and with human stories. Researchers make decisions about how to angle their vision on these places, depending on the interplay between their own interests and the grounded particularities of the site.*
>
> —Anne Haas Dyson & Celia Genishi, 2005, p. 12

The research design, curriculum, and teaching ideas for this project all derived from the local context where the study took place. The ethnically and linguistically diverse makeup of K–12 public school populations in the area, a major urban center in the Southwest, is representative of the dramatically shifting demographics occurring on a larger scale in schools across the country.

Jessica selected the school site, Libertad High School, to conduct the study for three reasons. First, it is one of the largest urban public high schools located in the largest school district in Arizona.

Second, besides serving a large student population, the school's student body is ethnically and linguistically diverse and low-income. The city's population is 64% non-Hispanic White, 26.4% Hispanic or Latino, 3.5% Black, 2.4% American Indian, 1.9% Asian, .4% Hawaiian or Pacific Islander, and 1.4% identify as two or more races (U.S. Census Bureau, 2012). Forty-one low-income, multiethnic 12th-grade students took part in the workshop.

Third, Jessica maintains a close research and mentoring relationship with the high school through professional development, teacher training for pre- and in-service secondary English teachers, and the NWP program, and she has formed a bidirectional relationship with the high school and, more specifically, its English department. This connection allowed her to begin a conversation with the two English teachers who participated in the study, Sarah and Dan. After establishing this relationship, conducting observations in English classes throughout a semester, and attending multiple department planning meetings during the school year as well as meetings with the cooperating teachers over the summer, Jessica decided to conduct the college admission essay study in this school setting.

LIBERTAD HIGH SCHOOL

Libertad High School serves students from 10th through 12th grade (the names of the school, students, and classroom teachers are pseudonyms). Located on a narrow neighborhood street, the school is reminiscent of an old shopping center. It is set back from the street and surrounded by a high chain-link fence and parking lots. The building is aging, with a desert-beige exterior and few windows. The campus has few trees and little greenery, and mobile classrooms dot the fence at the back of campus. A courtyard resides between the central offices and the classroom buildings; students often gather here during passing periods and lunch hour. The school is surrounded by busy streets, modest one-story homes, and sports fields where youth and their families regularly play soccer.

The school community is ethnically and linguistically diverse, with a large population of working-class and low-income Hispanic and Caucasian students and a sizable population of African American students. According to the state's school report card, more than 50% of the students are "economically disadvantaged," and more than 25% of the students live in homes where a language other than English is spoken (Arizona Department of Education [ADE], 2008).

Libertad also has the highest population of Native American students in the district and serves students from the 21 Native American nations of the state. More than 295,000 Native Americans live in Arizona and more than a quarter of the state's land is reservation and tribal community land (U.S. Census, 2010). Because of the diverse makeup of the school, researchers at the local university and teachers at the high school have teamed up to offer curriculum devoted to Native American history and literature and to conduct research examining the literacy practices of Native American students (Kinloch & San Pedro, forthcoming; San Pedro, 2011). Dan described the school population in this way:

> Libertad has a diverse student population in terms of culture, ethnicity, and social economic status. We have students who come from wealthy families who have been in the area for a long time and students who are the opposite and come from pretty difficult circumstances. We have a lot of first-generation students who are recent immigrants to the United States, trying to get a foothold. Libertad has a positive relationship with the community, but it

TABLE 3.1. Breakdown of Students' GPA and Primary Language

	Class A	Class B
Number of Participants	19	22
Mean GPA	3.18*	3.36*
Primary Language		
English	58%	36%
Spanish	37%	54%
Spanish/English	5%	0%
Navajo/English	0%	5%
Tagalog	0%	5%

Note. One GPA was not reported in Class A and six were not reported in Class B.

does not have active parental support. The people who live around Libertad definitely look to the school as a resource and as a support for their children.

THE STUDENTS

Nineteen boys and 22 girls from two separate and regularly scheduled, tracked senior English classes participated in this workshop. These classes were offered to underperforming students in the school and were labeled "regular English." Students had been sorted into these classes prior to the study based on poor performance on statewide literacy assessments and/or low grade-point averages (GPAs). Twenty-nine of the 41 students self-identified as Latino (71%). Six of the 41 students self-identified as Anglo (15%), 3 as Native American (7%), 2 as African American (5%), and 1 as Asian American (2%).

Although the majority of the students had been previously classified as ELL, none of them were taking part in ELL programs at the time of the study and all were enrolled in regular English classes. Most of the students spoke Spanish as their first learned or primary language.

Fewer than 50% of the participants' parents had attended high school, and the majority of the participants were the first in their family to pursue higher education. None of the students had received instruction on writing the college admission essay prior to this study. (See Table 3.1 for additional information about the students.)

The students who participated in the workshop came from an array of backgrounds and drew from a variety of experiences for inspiration in their writing. Some students were basketball all-stars, soccer players, and gymnasts. Some students loved hip-hop music, comic books, mother-daughter bonding time, and extracurricular activities such as student council and choir. Even though each student was unique, with his or her own interests and hobbies, all had aspirations to attend and graduate from a post-secondary institution. Many, especially those whose parents were born in Mexico and were first-generation immigrants, hoped to be the first in their family to graduate from high school and go on to college. Others expressed concern over how they would pay for their education and knew they would need full-time work to support themselves.

During the workshop, the students' stories and personalities were constant reminders of why educators, like ourselves, do the work we do. The students' commitment to their education and desire to succeed in life, despite the fact that they had been labeled "underachieving," was inspiring. A few students, in particular, left lasting impressions:

a. Carmen—a Latina who wants to become a nurse so she can help others, and often plays the role of caretaker to her younger siblings while her mom works late nights and long hours
b. Cody—a Native American who was raised by his grandfather, speaks with a lisp, struggles with depression after the loss of his sister at the hands of a drunk driver, and wants to make movies one day
c. Cynthia—a Latina who honors and loves her mother, supports her father who was disabled from a work-related injury, and was 9 months pregnant when the workshop began and left school for the birth of her baby girl
d. Gisele—a Latina who works (and attends school) full-time to pay for gymnastics lessons her parents can't afford
e. Ramiro—a Latino who has a part-time job, bought his first car during the workshop, has nine siblings and a mother who is a migrant worker, and wants to be a doctor
f. Roxanna—a Latina who took the workshop more seriously than she let on, works at a clothing store after school, and felt exhausted from juggling work, school, friends, and family
g. Talia—a Latina student who wants to attend Brigham Young University and major in journalism, and whose mother passed away 6 months prior to the workshop
h. Tiana—a Navajo who wants to be a doctor so she can serve her local community on the Navajo reservation where she was raised
i. Victor—a tall Latino who plays basketball, married his high school sweetheart, and was expecting a baby at the time of the workshop.

THE TEACHERS

The teachers who took part in this study, Sarah and Dan, were generous in allowing access to their students and curriculum. It can be a challenge to open up a classroom and invite "outsiders" to take part in classroom activities. Sarah and Dan continually expressed how they wanted this workshop for their students and for their own teaching and knew that this project was, according to Dan, "a wonderful way to help students plan for and pursue post-secondary education." Both teachers had at least 5 years of experience teaching ethnically and linguistically diverse secondary students before this study took place. Sarah and Dan are both White and speak English as their first language. Dan is fluent in both Spanish and English and taught a few Spanish courses as well as English classes. At the time of the study, both teachers were in their mid-30s. Each teacher chose different roles in the workshop process. Sarah, the teacher for Class A, took on an observational role, while Dan, the teacher for Class B, chose a participatory co-teaching role. Both of these teachers were seasoned veterans in the classroom and had worked at Libertad High School for over 10 years combined. Sarah and Dan were also devoted to creating curriculum opportunities for their students to think about and plan for the future.

Sarah taught English to sophomores and seniors and she also ran the school's Advancement Via Individual Determination (AVID) program, a college preparatory program for students who may have missed academic opportunities, are historically underrepresented in colleges, or find themselves in the academic middle. Along with her work as a full-time teacher, Sarah taught evening composition courses at a local community college. She told Jessica in an informal conversation before class one morning, "I have two teenagers and I need extra money to help pay for their cars and college fund."

Sarah was a calm, soft-spoken, methodical, and dedicated instructor. She described herself as a "gentle and patient mother figure." Her room was decorated with student-generated poetry, art, photography, and writing. She told Jessica that her best teaching quality is her ability to connect with students who struggle academically or socially.

Dan, who taught English and Spanish, was a vivacious, fast-paced, and enthusiastic teacher. His room was lined with posters from countries around the world. Dan rarely sat still and often circled the room to check in with students (and us) to ensure that everyone felt supported. He and his wife had just adopted a baby, and he was overjoyed about becoming a father. In an interview with Arturo, the lead research assistant during the data collection process, after the completion of the workshop, Dan shared that his best qualities as a teacher were his "passion for the subject matter, love of languages, fast pace, and rigorous expectations." Dan was also a published fiction writer who loved to write alongside his students.

THE RESEARCH AND TEACHING TEAM

The research and teaching team included the classroom teachers, Sarah and Dan; the principal investigator, Jessica; and four research assistants, Meredith, Arturo, Cynthia, and Sara. In the first stages of the study, Arturo—a Latino man, Cynthia—an African American woman, and Sara—a White woman, assisted with the preparation, development, and implementation of the workshop and the data collection. Arturo helped build strong relationships with the classroom teachers, administrators, and school secretarial, security, and parking staff through open and ongoing face-to-face, email, and phone communication. He assisted with the development and teaching of all the skill lessons, collected and organized the writing samples, and assisted in interviewing the teachers and students. Arturo had substantial experience teaching high school English in the Southwest before moving on to pursue his doctoral work in English education. At the time the study took place, Arturo was in the second year of his doctoral studies. He is bilingual and often spoke Spanish in writing conferences with students and shared his expertise as a first-generation college student throughout the workshop. Cynthia, also a veteran teacher with years of experience working with ethnically and linguistically diverse secondary students in the southern region of the United States, was in her first year of doctoral studies in English education at the time the study took place. She served as a research assistant alongside Arturo and helped develop and teach skill lessons, conferenced with students about their writing progress, took field notes, and assisted in the collection of writing models for the skill lessons. Sara was in her last year of undergraduate studies at the time the study took place. She was studying in the honors college at the local university and pursuing a degree in English. She worked on this project the spring and summer semesters before the workshop began and the semester the workshop was implemented. Sara collected examples of successful college admission essays from 50 first-year college students attending colleges and universities from around the country and from college admission guidebooks. She researched the local bills and laws connected to the teaching of ethnic studies and teaching undocumented students that had passed in the state at the time the study was taking place to understand the ways ethnically and linguistically diverse secondary students could still find support for and access to scholarships for pursuing higher education despite the intense political backdrop. Sara also organized a panel of ethnically and linguistically diverse undergraduate students to attend one of the college admission essay workshop sessions and share their experiences and advice for preparing for and getting into college. Sara wrote about her experience as a research assistant on this project as the focus of her honors thesis. All three of these research assistants departed after the data collection phase of this research to graduate or move on to course work and other research projects.

The second author, Meredith, joined this project as a research assistant after the workshop was complete. Jessica recruited her for this role because of her interest in examining secondary writing practices in ethnically and linguistically diverse settings and her former experience teaching English language arts. Meredith was a doctoral student in English education with 2 years of English language arts teaching experience in a secondary school in the southern region of the United States. Meredith initially assisted Jessica and Arturo with the interviews, and over time assisted Jessica with the organization and coding of writing samples, data analysis, and overall write-up of the findings. All members of the research team have assisted Jessica with presentations of this work at local, national, and international conferences.

All four of the research assistants are former high school English teachers and have firsthand experience working with ethnically and linguistically diverse, low-income student populations in urban settings in states across the country, including California, Indiana, Kentucky, Texas, Virginia, and Arizona. (Sara, the undergraduate student, was training to become an English teacher.) The research assistants met with Jessica once a week over the course of a year during the planning, implementation, and follow-up stages of the study.

Although everyone involved in the study hailed from different backgrounds and lived experiences, they came together for a common purpose: to learn the many reasons why the college admission essay matters and how to write a successful essay. The students specifically wanted to gain a better sense of what it takes to apply and gain admission to a postsecondary institution. Sarah and Dan wanted not only to provide their students with a real world writing task that could do this, but they also wanted to think about and participate in writing instruction in ways they had not done previously. The research team wanted to explore the teaching of a real world, gate-opening writing genre with a group of ethnically and linguistically diverse students and learn more about conducting writing research in secondary classrooms. Through the collaborative effort of the students, teachers, and researchers, the story of a real world and gate-opening workshop began to unfold.

CHAPTER 4

Demystifying the College Admission Essay Genre

I am a girl who will do anything to be someone in life. I want to have a career and make my parents proud. In this workshop, I learned that when I put all my effort into writing something that matters to me and helps me move closer to achieving my life goals, then my work really shines.

—Roxanna, 12th-grade student, written reflection

Roxanna, a student from Dan's class, describes in this written reflection a sentiment shared by many of her classmates about the way the college admission essay workshop aligned with her future goals. She realized that she is more invested in her writing when she sees a clear connection between a writing task and her next life steps. The purpose of this chapter is to offer insight into the specific curricular and teaching choices involved in designing and implementing a real world, gate-opening writing workshop so teachers and researchers may draw from these pages to create similar opportunities for their students. This chapter provides:

a. an overview of the college admission essay genre
b. the key components of the college admission essay workshop
c. examples of student writing produced in the workshop
d. extensions and professional resources for teaching the college admission essay.

THE IMPORTANCE OF THE COLLEGE ADMISSION ESSAY

The college admission essay, personal statements, application letters, and other similar writing tasks hold a great deal of power. However, as with so many writing genres students encounter in their transition from high school to college and from college to the workplace, an air of mystery prevails. As reading skills and literary analysis become increasingly important in the classroom due to high-stakes testing, many students are not provided opportunities to engage in writing tasks that are of any-substance, depth, or complexity (Applebee & Langer, 2009). This is disconcerting for students who aspire to attend college and will encounter challenging and complex writing tasks in their college courses, as well as for those students who want solid-paying jobs with high literacy demands (American Diploma Project, 2004).

What is even more concerning is that low-income, second language, and ethnic minorities often miss out on these rich writing opportunities and are more likely to be exposed to skill and drill learning in the classroom due to issues of sorting and tracking as well as ongoing political pressures and scripted curriculum (Kohn, 1999; Oakes & Wells, 1998). Rather than engaging in a rich curriculum that helps them become productive members of the community and find success in college, the workplace, and beyond, far too many ethnically and linguistically diverse youth are immersed in remediated curriculum that is designed to help them perform well on standardized tests. However, engaging in gate-opening writing tasks helps students begin to understand how these tasks function both rhetorically and socially, and provides them with a form of currency that they may use to access and participate in various institutions of power, including universities, businesses, and community organizations.

Most colleges and universities in the United States, Canada, Great Britain, Australia, and other countries around the world evaluate students' admission applications using multiple criteria. According to the National Association for College Admission Counseling (NACAC, 2008), these criteria include:

a. ability to pay
b. recommendations from high school counselors and teachers
c. interviews
d. high school grade-point averages
e. high school class rank
f. evidence of extracurricular activities
g. admission test scores
h. quality of a written essay.

The college admission essay is one example of a real world, gate-opening genre form because it is a basic requirement of many higher education institutions that has real consequences. That is, it is clear that this genre of writing serves as a gate through which students must pass to gain admittance to many universities and colleges around the world.

Post-secondary-bound high school students typically write these essays during the first semester of their senior year as part of the college application process. Some students seek assistance from English teachers, guidance counselors, or parents, whereas others write the essay on their own. This genre is especially tough for students who are in the process of learning English or whose parents do not speak English and may not be able to offer feedback on the essay. To complicate matters, 12th-grade students generally write these essays for a particular yet unknown audience: college admission officers and admission committees. If students do not have a clear understanding of the audience, it is challenging to compose an essay that meets that audience's needs and expectations.

For many post-secondary institutions, the admission essay is the only opportunity to learn about applicants personally. It also is one of the only ways these institutions are exposed to students' writing prior to admission. The importance of these essays is evidenced by the large university systems in the United States that have adopted common prompts and instructions that help define the genre. For example, the University of California requires all applicants to write two personal statements based on prompts like these (UC Regents, 2010):

a. Describe the world you come from—for example, your family, community, or school—and tell us how your world has shaped your dreams and aspirations.
b. Tell us about a personal quality, talent, accomplishment, contribution, or experience that is important to you. What about this quality or accomplishment makes you proud and how does it relate to the person you are? (UC Regents, 2010, para 3 & 5)

The importance of admission essays has increased recently as more colleges and universities have opted not to require SAT scores as one of their criteria for evaluating students' admission applications. In 1993, only 14% of colleges thought the essay was of "considerable importance," but by 2006, 28% considered the essay to be a significant admission factor, and that number continues to grow (NACAC, 2008; National Center for Education Statistics [NCES], 2009). Currently, 414, or approximately 15%, of 4-year degree-granting institutions in the United States use the Common Application, which is accepted at private and public schools around the country (n.d.b.). The Common Application (n.d.a.) essay prompt is open-ended and allows students to choose from six essay topics:

a. significant experience, risk, or ethical dilemma
b. issue of local, national, or international concern
c. significant person
d. important character from a text
e. personal experience that represents diversity
f. topic of choice.

Although numerous guides have been published on how to write successful college admission essays (see Gelband, Kubale, & Schorr, 1986; The Harvard Independent, 2002), there is little empirical support for the efficacy of these methods (Samway, 2006). Of the writing workshops and research studies that focus on ethnically and linguistically diverse secondary students, none examines the impact of features-based instruction on improving the writing quality of college admissions essays (Graham & Perin, 2007a). This is where our workshop comes in.

The college admission essay workshop took place during the fall semester and involved explicit teaching, modeling, and practicing of writing skills connected to the college admission essay genre. All instruction was provided during the students' regularly scheduled, 55-minute English class and was offered 2 to 3 days a week over the course of 6 weeks, for a total of 13 class sessions (see Appendix A for a detailed schedule created by Jessica). Students received instruction from members of the teaching and research team and from their classroom teachers. All curriculum for the workshop was created and designed by Jessica, with assistance from Arturo and Cynthia, the two doctoral students who assisted with the teaching of the workshop.

OVERVIEW OF THE COLLEGE ADMISSION ESSAY WORKSHOP

There were three phases of the workshop process, including the introduction to the workshop, teaching key genre elements, and the conclusion to the workshop. Students wrote three drafts (one draft for each stage of the workshop) of their essays over the course of the workshop: an initial draft, a working or instructional draft developed as part of the curriculum unit, and a third and final draft. Students wrote the initial draft during the second class session of the writing workshop, prior to instruction on the key genre elements. This draft was an essay responding to a written prompt from the Common Application (n.d.a.), which is also the required prompt for one of the major universities in the state where the study took place. The research and teaching team wanted to collect an initial writing sample to gain an understanding of students' strengths and weaknesses in writing this genre prior to instruction. In the second phase of the workshop, students received instruction on the key genre elements for the instructional essay. For this essay, students chose from three open-ended essay topics taken from the Common Application prompts, which required students to write about personal experience. For example, one of the questions asked students to evaluate a significant experience, achievement, or risk they have taken, or an ethical dilemma they have faced and its impact (The Common Application, n.d.b.). The third and final draft was completed at the conclusion of the workshop. It was important to give students multiple opportunities to write and revise in this genre and see what challenges presented themselves with this type of writing. The three drafts also gave the research team a chance to gauge student progress over the course of the workshop.

Each class session of the college admission essay workshop consisted of seven steps:

a. a skill lesson to introduce and define the genre element or skill
b. use of models/examples
c. opportunity for students to practice skill(s)
d. opportunity for students to share writing
e. opportunity for students to practice skill(s) again as part of a college admission essay project in progress
f. opportunity for students to receive feedback from peers or instructors
g. opportunity for students to revise.

Although each session was structured in this way, the research and teaching team used examples of successful writing strategies, conferenced with students, and continually revised curriculum and lessons to address students' questions, strengths, and needs. Because the research and teaching team wanted the workshop to be dynamic and not prescriptive, it was important to mold the curriculum around students' unique needs.

The following sections cover the introduction to the workshop, the key genre elements for the college admission essay, and the conclusion of the workshop. Excerpts of student writing appear throughout the description and analysis of the different stages of the workshop to illustrate students' writing before and after the explicit skill lessons devoted to this gate-opening genre.

INTRODUCING THE WORKSHOP

In the first phase of the workshop (Days 1–4), the research and teaching team spent time getting to know students in both classes through writing, discussion, questionnaires, and surveys. These days were also devoted to introducing students to the college admission essay as a genre so they could think about the purpose, audience, and context for this writing task. On the first day of the workshop, the research and teaching team distributed one questionnaire and one survey. The questionnaire asked students to respond to a series of questions regarding their experience with and understanding of the college admission essay genre. The questionnaire invited students to answer questions such as:

a. Please describe any prior experience writing the college admission essay.
b. Describe your feelings associated with applying to college and writing admissions essays.
c. What would you like help with in the process of writing college admission essays?

The survey was a writing self-efficacy survey and asked students to rank their confidence in a variety of areas. Jessica derived the questionnaire from Bandura (1986) and Shell et al. (1995). This questionnaire consisted of 15 questions connected to facets of writing associated with the college admission essay genre in a response format of an 11-point confidence Likert-like scale ranging from "not at all confident" to "completely confident." Seven of the survey questions asked students to note their confidence with particular genre elements of a college admission essay:

a. overall writing of a college admission essay,
b. understanding different parts of the college admission essay,
c. writing an introduction,
d. writing a conclusion,
e. using description,
f. sharing lived experiences,
g. audience awareness.

Five questions asked students about their confidence with general writing skills:

a. varying sentence structure,
b. expressing voice,

c. use of adjectives,
d. use of description,
e. writing about setting.

Three of the questions asked participants to rate their confidence with elements of the writing process, including:

a. asking for help with the essay,
b. revising their own essay,
c. revising someone else's essay.

This questionnaire was administered on the first day of the workshop with all participants and again at the end of the workshop on the last day.

Through their responses to the questionnaire and survey and in informal conversations, students described having no prior experience writing college admission essays, and many said they felt anxious or intimidated at the prospect. The research and teaching team used the first days of the workshop to understand students' perspectives and to plan curriculum based on their needs. For example, from the first day of the workshop, students expressed how college admission essay questions felt intimidating, like a "test" or a "trick," because they seem so open-ended and provide such a range of topic choice. The research and teaching team's goal was to provide students with access to some of the unwritten rules of the genre so they could think of the questions as part of a larger pattern rather than a test or a trick. The first days of the workshop were also devoted to pre-writing and brainstorming work as a way to warm up to the writing task as a whole and to think about the importance of choosing a strong writing topic.

Choosing a Strong Topic

An entire class (Day 3) was devoted to strategies for selecting strong essay topics. The research and teaching team began by pointing out how most college admission essay topics, regardless of their wording, fall into three general categories:

a. questions regarding the writer's interests,
b. questions regarding the writer's values and beliefs,
c. and questions regarding the writer's thought process (College Board, n.d.b.).

The research and teaching team then asked students to practice selecting a topic using a range of options taken directly from the Common

Application prompt. (Most colleges and universities that require college admission essays as part of their application process provide potential students with more than one essay question.) Examples of some options follow:

a. What experiences have led you to select your professional field and objective?
b. Does any attribute, quality, or skill distinguish you from everyone else? How did you develop this attribute?
c. Describe a character in fiction, a historical figure, or a creative work (as in art, music, science, and so on) that has had an influence on you, and explain that influence.
d. What was the most difficult time in your life, and why? How did your perspective on life change as a result of the difficulty?
e. In your opinion, what is the greatest challenge that your generation will face? What ideas do you have for dealing with this issue?

The research and teaching team wanted students to practice selecting successful topics for their writing for a real world audience, but this step created anxiety and uncertainty for many students. Through class discussion, students shared that they were not used to having the freedom to choose their topic and were unsure of their audience. For example, Marco spent half of one session staring at the questions until Dan asked him to articulate what he was thinking. He explained, "I am not sure what I am supposed to write about. This feels like a test. If I choose the wrong topic, I am doomed from the beginning." Other students, such as Tiana, shared Marco's feelings and felt the openness of the questions created too much freedom. Tiana explained, "I feel more comfortable when someone just tells me what I'm supposed to write about and then I can go ahead and write. If I have too many options, I feel out of control. . . . I'm not sure what they want me to say."

To help students like Marco and Tiana, the research and teaching team told them to go with their gut and choose a topic they knew something about and felt invested in right away. The research and teaching team also gave students permission at any time to change their topics if they felt stuck or uninspired. In a conversation with Jessica after class, Mariah shared her relief once she heard she could change her mind:

> I initially chose to write about community service because I was working on a scholarship that addressed this issue and I had already written a little bit on this topic previously. I thought it would be easy. Now, after writing a little bit, I realize I am sick of the subject

and I decided to make a change. It felt like a huge relief lifted off my shoulders to know I could start fresh with a new idea.

But not everyone struggled with picking a topic. Talia knew immediately that she wanted to write about the loss of her mom, and she stayed with this topic throughout the workshop. Although choosing her topic came easily, she felt less sure of the focus of her essay because the loss of her mom was such an overwhelming experience. She noted, "I feel like I could write a whole book about my mom and her impact on my life. I know I need to focus my story to make it fit the purpose of the piece." Victor explained that he quickly decided to write about feeling "trapped in my White skin" because he had always felt conflicted about being Latino and having very pale skin when all of his Latino friends have much darker skin. He shared, "I have more to say about this than anything else. I thought about what I wanted to write ahead of time and as I began brainstorming, more ideas came to mind and I knew I had a good match."

Pre-Writing

The research and teaching team encouraged students to take part in pre-writing and invention work to see if their initial topic ideas were a good fit (Day 3). Invention work is a step writers often take part in before formally drafting. For example, writers often brainstorm, prepare outlines, and collect and read materials related to their topic. The research and teaching team first modeled various brainstorming strategies, including mapping, webbing, outlining, or listing ideas. Then students chose one or two of these techniques to practice. Jenissa, for example, was torn between topic ideas so she quickly scribbled two lists. Her first list was titled "Social Worker (CPS)" and included the following quick phrases: "bad experience on the rez [reservation]" and "they [Child Protective Services] don't help like they need to." Her second list was titled "Baseball" and included a list of five key words: *practice, team, dad, pitching,* and *support*. She said she was torn between an extremely personal and heart-wrenching experience with abuse and, as she described it, "a much safer and more generic memory about playing baseball with my dad." Jenissa said she needed to figure out which topic felt most compelling to her as a writer. She also wanted to learn more about what a college admission officer would rather read. As the workshop progressed, however, Jenissa abandoned both ideas, along with a few that followed, to write instead about her relationship with her grandmother. She said the pre-writing "allowed me to try out ideas until one stuck."

Yobi used mapping and listing as forms of pre-writing. Unlike Jenissa, he knew immediately what he wanted to write about, but he wanted to experiment with different ways of thinking about the topic before drafting. The center of his map included his topic, "Mom's death," and he drew bubbles and arrows out from these central words to include key phrases to help him think about this life experience. He wrote, "Because I couldn't cry I no longer felt anything" and "I was eight." Below his map, Yobi created a list of 10 key words and phrases to help him think about the impact of his mother's death on his life:

a. the death
b. the feelings
c. why I couldn't cry
d. why I couldn't feel anything for a long time
e. how I look at life now
f. how I treat women
g. how I treat my grandma and elders
h. why I'm so sensitive
i. how I protect myself
j. who changed my way of life after the death.

During a writing conference, Yobi explained how mapping and listing not only helped him focus his topic but also served as an outline for his future essay.

What We Learned

After analyzing students' preliminary topic ideas and writing from the first few days of the workshop, the research and teaching team found that many had powerful life experiences to share; however, the writing did not exhibit many of the genre elements necessary to share these experiences effectively with a college admissions officer. Many of the initial essays were incomplete and lacked detail, description, and focus. As we reviewed the initial drafts, we anticipated the writing would be rough because students had not had time to revise and polish the pieces, but these writing samples gave us one way to gain a sense of students' needs and pinpoint specific strategies we could focus on to support their writing. For example, Rodrigo's 11-sentence, three-paragraph essay about the positive influence of his father began with the following lead: "In my life my dad has influenced me greatly. His teachings of working hard, progression, and never giving up has served me well up to this point. It has shaped and molded the person I am today." While Rodrigo's love and respect for his father were clear, his lead did not have the elements of a strong opening. It lacked a powerful quote or a series of questions or a compelling anecdote.

Many of the essays also lacked organization and audience awareness. Gisele's essay, for example, focused on the struggles and the triumphs she faced working and attending school full-time to pay for gymnastics lessons her unemployed parents cannot afford. Although the topic was intriguing and the essay included important details, the 20 essay sentences comprised a single paragraph. Phrases such as "when I'm hit with some obstacle" and "so being myself I found a job during the summer" illustrated the essay's inappropriate, informal tone. The issues the research and teaching team uncovered in Gisele's essay are emblematic of the issues discovered in the student essays as a whole, and suggested a need to discuss the importance of the key genre elements and teach them explicitly.

Getting to Know the Audience

After analyzing the students' initial essays, the research and teaching team decided to devote a class to understanding audience and purpose as a step toward successfully executing this real world, gate-opening genre (Day 4). Writing scholars such as Barry M. Kroll (1981) and José Brandão Carvalho (2002) have emphasized the importance of audience awareness and deemed it one of the major markers that separate novice from experienced writers. One aspect of what marks the college admission essay as a "gatekeeping" writing task for many students is that the audience is unknown.

Addressing Preconceived Notions. In the skill lesson on audience awareness, students responded to a set of brief brainstorming questions asking them to think about the rhetorical situation for the college admission essay, meaning the audience, purpose, topic, and context for this genre (see Figure 4.1).

As students completed their brainstorming questions, many said they imagined the audience of college admission officers as "old," "conservative," and "White." Cody, a highly verbal student who always sat in the front row, blurted out, "I've never thought about who ends up actually reading these essays. I just assumed they would wind up in some file somewhere." Lindsey, a quiet student, raised her hand to share, "When I think of college admission officers, I think of White men. I never picture anyone who looks or thinks like me." On her questionnaire, Lindsey wrote that her audience would most likely be a "42-year-old, upper-class, male professor with a Ph.D., and Caucasian." She also stated that this unknown reader would expect her to be "smart, well-rounded, and world-

FIGURE 4.1. Thinking About the Rhetorical Situation for the College Admission Essay

1. Purpose: What is the purpose of writing a college admission essay? Explain.
2. Genre: How would you categorize the college admission essay as a type of writing? (e.g., fiction, autobiographical story, news article, review, letter to the editor, rhetorical analysis, criticism, persuasive essay). Explain.
3. Audience: Who do you imagine is the audience for the college admission essay? Describe using details (e.g., social class, age, gender).
4. Topic: What do you plan to write about? Why is this topic important to you and why do you think it will be important your audience?

ly." Many students pictured "men in suits and ties with white hair and glasses" reading their essays with a critical eye.

Once students shared their preconceived notions of the audience, the research and teaching team talked about the role of college admission officers and the purpose of the college admissions office. It was not possible to provide a concrete description of the admission officers, since they are diverse individuals and little information about them as a group is released publicly. However, the research and teaching team did tell students that their audience would most likely be employed by the university, highly educated, older than they are, and invested in recruiting and accepting new students who best exemplify the school's mission.

Understanding Context. The research and teaching team also wanted students to understand how many post-secondary institutions are similar to businesses seeking new customers. Our goal was to show students how universities provide information about what they value through their promotional materials and how this might offer some insight into the school's mission and expectations for students.

The research and teaching team showed students examples of college admission websites so they could see how schools advertise themselves. They noticed the kinds of photos, quotes, and documents schools use to promote athletics, campus life, diversity, and quality education. Some of the sites include:

a. University of Texas (http://bealonghorn.utexas.edu/freshmen/)—contains detailed information on everything from life in Austin, where the school is located, to profiles of current students
b. University of California at Berkeley (http://students.berkeley.edu/admissions/index.asp)—lists its acceptance statistics and the average SAT score average and GPA of incoming freshmen

c. Emory University in Atlanta (http://www.emory.edu/home/prospective/index.html)—offers a number of quick links to the university's social media pages to help students get acquainted with the school community.

Understanding a college or university's context, student body, size, academic programs, and recreational activities is a way to gain insight into the school's culture and community, and for the purposes of our workshop, it served as a way to give students a sense of agency when writing the admission essay. Rather than thinking of their audience as "people we can't relate to," "judges and critics," or "old and conservative and not at all like me," students gained more confidence and voice regarding the writing task when they realized that as students, they were the customers writing for real people.

Many students had never thought about finding a school that was a good fit with their values, culture, academic and social goals, and financial means. Understandably, many likened success with the application and acceptance process to a shot in the dark. Mariah said, "I never realized that I can make choices about the kind of place I end up going. I didn't really think I had a say in this until now." Her comment highlights the importance of demystifying colleges' and universities' similarities and differences, students' role and influence in the admission process, and the fact that they are writing an essay for a real audience.

Lesson Results

As students started brainstorming topics and drafting their second essays in the first weeks of the workshop, the research and teaching team reminded them to think about audience and purpose. After reading the working drafts of students' essays, the research and teaching team noticed how some students made decisions about topic choice, voice, and their overarching theme based on audience awareness. For example, Maritza's initial draft describing her mother's impact on her life began as follows:

> My mother, Maria, is the person that has influenced me. She is a big part of my life and I'm really glad to have her. She influenced me by telling me about her life and not letting me go through the things she had to go through. She never had the opportunity to finish high school until she got older she went to take classes to finish it. She had showed me and encouraged me to never give up my education because without it my life would be full of struggles.

Maritza initially felt her first topic was important and compelling, but after participating in the audience awareness workshop, brainstorming ideas, and talking to classmates, she realized she wanted to expand upon her topic to show the way her mother's influence has led to her academic accomplishments and participation in extracurricular activities. After having a chance to think through and receive feedback on her original ideas, she realized that expanding her topic to share her academic accomplishments and extracurricular interests would help address the university audience and purpose more explicitly. She wanted to attend Brigham Young University and she realized that the academic enrichment programs she had participated in all connected well to the mission of the university:

> How many different ways can you get into a university? Many people just focus on their grades but not me. I've always been told "Maritza, you're a very smart girl and you can get far." Those words motivate me to try to get into a university. I didn't focus only on my grades though. I always signed up for programs that will help me get into a university. Right now I am in the Hispanic Mother Daughter Program, the AVID Program and also the Reach Program. All three of these programs have showed me different ways to achieve my goals.

While some students, like Maritza, chose to change topics as a result of the skill lesson on audience awareness, most expressed how the lesson made them feel more confident in the topics they had selected. Gladys explained how growing up with overprotective parents has influenced her:

> I realize I shouldn't feel embarrassed writing about my topic because it reflects who I am. I am going to write about how my family has sheltered me and kept me from taking part in activities with my peers my whole life and how this has shaped who I am as a student, young woman, and person.

KEY GENRE ELEMENTS OF THE COLLEGE ADMISSION ESSAY

As mentioned, students worked on the second working draft of the essay while receiving instruction—specifically, several skill lessons on key genre elements of the college admission essay. Jessica and Sara derived these elements by collecting and examining as many examples of this type of

FIGURE 4.2. Key Genre Elements of the College Admission Essay

1. *Selecting a strong writing topic*: Consider personal experiences, issues of importance, or influential individuals while taking into account the expectations of college admission officers.
2. *Writing for the appropriate audience*: Consider the unfamiliar audience of college admission officers.
3. *Writing an effective introduction*: Consider effective techniques for a lead, such as beginning with a powerful quote, a series of questions, or a compelling anecdote.
4. *Using description*: Use vivid details to show, not tell, anecdotes from life events.
5. *Writing the "So What?"*: Step outside the narrative to emphasize the significance of the particular topic and lesson learned. Share why the story represents the writer's unique interests and potential contributions to a university community.
6. *Making outside connections*: Embed outside texts, events, or ideas; explicitly reference outside sources.
7. *Writing an effective conclusion*: End on a powerful and memorable note to stand apart from other applicants.

writing as possible prior to the workshop. A thorough review of successful examples of college admission essays provided insight into some of the most common features of this type of writing. After an extensive online and book search, Jessica and Sara collected 50 examples of college admission essays from college students who had applied and been accepted to colleges and universities in Arizona, Maine, California, Texas, Oregon, and Washington. These essays were read and coded to find specific elements and repeated patterns used for this genre. Several elements emerged from our analysis (see Figure 4.2).

These genre elements became the instructional focus of the workshop. The working draft of the essay served as an opportunity for students to take part in a process approach to learning about this genre (Atwell, 1987; Singer, 2006). For this draft, students were guided through different steps of writing an admission essay from invention to drafting to revising.

Writing a Successful Introduction

One of the first genre elements taught in the workshop was the introduction (Day 5). As part of the opening questionnaire, which students filled out at the beginning of the workshop, many expressed concerns about "how to get started" and how to "format" their essays. Students

FIGURE 4.3. Lead Options and Directions for Using Them

Option 1

Question(s) or dialogue: Ask one or a series of questions to catch readers' attention. Examples of question stems include: Do you remember _____? Did you know _____? Have you ever thought about _____? Or start your essay with an action or dialogue that immediately takes readers into the story you want to share. Keep in mind: The questions and dialogue should relate to your topic.

Option 2

A compelling anecdote: Open with a small story that personalizes the essay topic. It may introduce who you are as a unique individual, pose the thesis or dilemma that controls your argument, or provide insight into your interests and values.

Option 3

A powerful quote: Begin with a quote from a conversation, song lyric, poem, statistic, or historical fact, or an old saying. Make sure the quote is not a dictionary definition or a cliché. Once you select the quote, be sure to show readers in the opening paragraph that follows the quote how it relates to your overall message.

also worried about the rhetorical situation; they feared that they might not be able to write well enough for college admission officers. Explicit teaching of the introduction helped allay some of their fears.

Consider Effective Techniques for a Lead. The research and teaching team first provided sample introductions from the set of essays Jessica and Sara had collected and analyzed prior to the study to determine key genre features for the workshop. In the samples, many of the writers used particular strategies to begin their pieces, and the research and teaching team wanted to make these transparent for students. Students also had the opportunity to practice these strategies in their writing, so after the team shared these models with the students, students were then given three possible strategies to practice, along with tips for approaching these different leads (see Figure 4.3). Students were also reminded that successful leads are almost always brief and work to set up the essay topic.

Enrique practiced all three options and decided the lead that seemed "the most natural and just clicked" was the one he had begun with a quote from Tupac Shakur:

> "Through every dark night there is a brighter day." This famous quote by Tupac Shakur is one I live by. I look up to many famous people who have been successful despite starting out with nothing.

> I like reading quotes and motivational speeches from Tupac, Michael Jordan, and Donald Trump because they all found ways of overcoming hardship. It has always been a challenge for me to focus on school work being the youngest male in a Mexican family with six kids and with two parents who have very limited schooling. My dad has a second grade education and my mom a sixth grade education. Both of my parents went to school in Mexico and came to the United States as very young adults. Even though my parents did not stay in school and despite many challenges I have faced, education has become a big part of who I am.

Students were given multiple opportunities throughout the workshop to practice writing and revising the college admission essay introduction, and expressed enthusiasm after learning this genre element. In a post-workshop interview, Victor explained to Jessica that learning new strategies for writing an introduction made a big difference in his overall writing. Below is a brief excerpt from his interview:

> *Jessica*: What did you find most useful about the overall college admission essay workshop?
>
> *Victor*: The lesson on how to get started in my essay helped me the most. Sometimes I have a hard time getting started and I have a hard time ending, but my middles are usually all right. I am tired of my basic way of writing. I always write papers using "First of all, second of all . . .". I want to learn to mix it up. Until now, I have always started and ended my writing using a formula my teachers had given me. I don't like formulas. It feels too forced and basic. I liked having more freedom and choice to try different ways of getting started. Formulas are so square. I am not square. It is important to have options. No one has ever shown me these writing options before.

In an informal conversation after the skill lesson on introductions, Victor shared how he felt the skill lesson gave him "ways to help my ideas flow."

Lesson Results. By learning ways of approaching the introduction to this genre, many students' leads showed marked improvement. Consider Carola's introduction to her initial essay. She simply listed several areas of academic interest and then briefly described her interest in reading:

> Some of my academic interests are reading, English, and science. I enjoy reading during my free time because I sometimes get so

> involved in the book and I forget where I am. Other times it feels like the story is real. I like to read all sorts of books from fantasy to non-fiction. As long as it's a good book, I'll read it.

After Carola had participated in the skill lesson on writing an effective introduction, she used vivid description to help introduce her father's impact on her personal growth:

> It seemed like he was always in a bad mood. When he had a bad day at work he would let steam out on us, when we hadn't done anything to deserve it. It was as if we could never make him happy. He always found ways to yell at us and make us feel bad. My dad never seemed to feel proud of me and I remember the many nights I cried myself to sleep wishing I didn't have a dad.

Carola not only switched the focus of her essay in this revised draft, but her writing became more fluid, descriptive, and compelling. She made the shift from listing her interests in a general and impersonal way to diving into the difficult story of her relationship with her father.

Izzy's first introduction, like Carola's, was more general than personal:

> My mom has had a positive influence on me. I am the youngest of three children and probably the one who spends the most time with our mom. I am the only one to have lived with her after she and my father got divorced. I appreciate every moment I spend with my mom because I know when it is time to move out on my own I will never find as much love and care as she has given me.

After the skill lesson, Izzy revised her introduction to reveal how she grew up in a challenging environment but thrived because of her mother's love and support:

> Most homes have a father, a mother, and children living under one roof. Unfortunately, that wasn't the case for me. After my mom and dad got a divorce, I lived only with my mom. I have lived this way for about twelve years now. For those first nine years, my dad never tried contacting us. At first I didn't know why, but as I got older I didn't care anymore. I was happy just having my mom around. Many people think I need a father figure in my life, but that wasn't necessary for me. My mom filled both sets of shoes.

Izzy's revised introduction illustrates growth in a number of ways. First, every sentence in her first introduction other than the first began in with "I" and provided little to no detail. The second draft incorporates more sentence variety and more personal connection. In the revised introduction after the skill lesson, Izzy lets her reader in on the reality of growing up with a single mother and having little to no contact with her father. Her introduction established her connection to her mom, her growing independence, and her strength as a young woman. The skill lesson gave students strategies to more effectively tell their stories. Next, the research and teaching team taught a brief skill lesson reminding students of the importance of using description in their writing (Day 6).

Using Description

In many of the students' initial essays, they "told" about significant people or events in their lives, but they did not "show" these using description. For example, Jenissa discussed the importance of family, but offered few details. She wrote,

> Ever since I can remember I have always been around my family. Growing up around them has definitely influenced me. They are always there when I need them, they are constantly teaching, and having younger members I learned responsibility.

Although Jenissa's love for her family could make for an interesting essay topic, the research and teaching team wanted to help her move beyond summarizing to make her essay stand out from others.

In this skill lesson, the research and teaching team provided students with multiple examples of college admission essays as well as poems and nonfiction pieces that either modeled effective use of description or emphasized the importance of using this strategy in writing (Hillocks, 2006; Lamott, 1994). The research and teaching team also used a lesson from Chapter 4 of Hillocks's (2007) *Narrative Writing*, on incorporating detail and figurative language. In this chapter, Hillocks explains that "the most important quality of effective stories is concrete detail. Specific details allow readers to see scenes in their own minds as they read" (p. 43). Hillocks emphasizes how writing with description can be challenging for young writers because the process of incorporating descriptive language into writing requires a number of steps and key decisions:

> Writers have to remember or imagine what it is they want to portray, search their memories for words to do it, arrange the words in effective syntax, evaluate the effort by comparing it with the vision in their mind, perhaps search for additional or different words or different ways to use them, write those down, and evaluate the effort again. (p. 43)

FIGURE 4.4. Using More Description

Descriptive writing is all about the difference between showing and telling in your writing.

Telling: The car is parked in front of the house.
Showing: The red, convertible sport car, with the new rims and fresh paint, is parked comfortably in front of the two-story house with the huge front yard.

The best way to work on descriptive writing is to ask yourself questions based upon your senses:

What can you see?
What can you taste?
What can you smell?
What can you hear?
What can you touch?

Then ask yourself questions that help you add vivid language. You can even make comparisons. Use as many similes or metaphors as possible.

What color is it?
What does it look like?
What does it remind you of?
What can you compare it to?

Practice

Try expanding on these sentences:

The girl cried.

The horse kicked the man.

The iPod played a song.

The research and teaching team wanted to give students a chance to learn the different steps Hillocks refers to in the above quote for incorporating description into their college admission essays. Arturo taught a short skill lesson on writing with description and invited students to practice using the five senses in their writing (see Figure 4.4).

Many students, like Jenissa, said they had taken part in lessons about using description in their writing in prior English classes; however, Jenissa also said in a writing conference with Jessica that it was helpful to "be reminded through this skill lesson that this kind of detail needs to go into the college admission essay because I had forgotten to add any details in my first draft." Jenissa used strategies from the skill lesson to retell her story with more detail. She wrote about learning to heed her grandmother's advice after she passed away:

> I can still picture her standing in front of the old comforting house in the red hills of New Mexico. The day I got the news she was in the hospital, I didn't know what to think or how to react. I sat on my bed in my room frozen with shock. I knew traveling eight hours to Santa Fe, New Mexico would surely affect my schoolwork. What I didn't know was just how much. Slowly my grades started slipping and my attitude towards school was no longer positive.

After taking part in the skill lesson on description, Jenissa's essay began to take shape. She added more descriptive language such as "comforting house" and "red hills of New Mexico," and she also focused her essay for clarity. She decided to write about her grandmother specifically rather than her family in general. Another student, Victoria, wrote her initial essay about her aunt, and, in it, she summarized a story about her childhood naptime: "My aunt used to take naps with me in the afternoons when I was young and I remember wetting the bed. She simply comforted me and never grew angry or upset." The description of the same story in Victoria's final essay was more nuanced and fluent:

> I lay there scared and embarrassed. My aunt cuddled up next to me. I hesitated to move. I was afraid my aunt would wake up angry at me for wetting the bed. Just when I thought my nap couldn't get worse, my aunt's blue eyes darted open. At first I thought she looked mad, but a smile slowly crept across her sweet face.

Victoria crafted her sentences to provide the reader a clearer picture of her aunt's reaction and comforting presence. Revisions such as these allowed students to more eloquently portray life experiences through their essays.

Writing a Successful "So What?"

As Thomas Newkirk (1997) argues in *The Performance of Self in Student Writing*, when students write personal statements or narratives, like the college admission essay, they are performing their identity in a way they think the audience will engage with or relate to. This means there must always be a point in the essay where the writer steps away from the story and speaks directly to the reader to make a case in the narrative for why he or she should gain admission to a college or university. Jessica called this the "So What?" section of the essay.

To explain this element to students, the research and teaching team told them that this was the part of the essay where, as writers, they needed to move back from the story and describe the lessons learned or the reason the story resonated in their lives. The "So What?" is the place in the college admission essay where the writer must do more than share personal experience: They must connect to an outside audience (see Figure 4.5). This is also a place in the essay where the writer shifts from telling a story to persuading the reader why the story matters. The "So What?" skill lesson invited students to answer a series of questions to reflect upon and articulate the overarching message in their essays.

Explaining Why Your Story Matters. Making this rhetorical shift was challenging for students. Many had experience writing personal stories in their English classes, not writing why these experiences mattered to others. In fact, students told us time and again that it was hard to believe that their stories would have meaning for or make a difference to anyone beyond family members. This was a place in the workshop where the research and teaching team chose to slow down and take the time to conference with students individually to give suggestions for reflecting on their lived experience with certitude.

In a writing conference, Gabriela shared her initial essay, which described the positive influence of her coworker, Guillermo, at an animal shelter. Gabriela's piece focused on Guillermo's story of hard work and persistence; therefore, the reader gained no understanding of Gabriela as a person or why Guillermo made a difference to her. In her conference, Gabriela shared how she had struggled her entire life with low self-esteem and paralyzing shyness. She explained how Guillermo was the first person she had spent time with who was outgoing, independent, and content. It became clear that Guillermo had served as a model for Gabriela, helping her see that she could begin to trust herself and her own voice. Taking time to conference gave Gabriela a chance to articulate aloud what she was hoping to get across in her writing and helped her realize she had left out important information. She returned to her essay and added details to the conclusion of her essay to show how her friendship with Guillermo had changed her perspective:

> Guillermo has taught me to accept myself, which has raised my self-esteem. I am no longer painfully shy at the shelter and enjoy talking to the new volunteers and workers. Guillermo has shown me that everyone is different and that our differences do not matter. What matters is learning to accept yourself.

Another student, Richard, wrote the first part of his essay about the positive impact his girlfriend has had on his life. Although he attempted

FIGURE 4.5. Skill Lesson: Finding Your "So What?"

Step 1

Spend 5 minutes reviewing all of the notes, outline, and brainstorming you have written so far. Let your head swim with information.

Step 2

Clear your desk of everything but a notebook. Remove all your notes and sources. You won't use these while doing the rest of this exercise. Trust that you'll remember what's important.

Step 3

Fast write about your topic for 8 minutes. Explain how your thinking about this topic has evolved. When you first thought about this project, what did you think? Then what happened, and what happened after that? What were your preconceptions about your topic? Have they changed? If so, how?

This is an open-ended fast write. Don't let the writing stall. What questions do you have about writing a college admission essay? What ideas do you have? What do you want help with?

Step 4

Skip a few lines on your page. Write "Moments, Stories, People, and Scenes." Now fast write for another 5 minutes. This time, focus on more specific case studies, situations, people, experiences, observations, and so on that stand out in your mind about your essay topic. Keep writing for the whole 5 minutes.

Step 5

Skip a few more lines. For 10 minutes, quickly write a dialogue between you and someone else connected to your essay topic—a friend, a teacher, someone with an opposing perspective. Don't plan the dialogue. Just begin with the question most commonly asked about your topic, and take the conversation from there, writing both parts of the dialogue.

Step 6

Finally, skip a few more lines and write "So What?" in your notebook. Now spend a few minutes trying to summarize the most important thing you think people should understand about your topic based on what you've learned so far. How has this experience impacted you? What can you tell your reader about yourself that they need to know to understand the person you are? Distill these comments down to a paragraph. This may be hard, but it's important. Remember, you can change your mind later.

to share his enthusiasm and deep love for her, his piece lacked cohesion and a clear purpose: "Now you might ask how one girl who isn't even a member of my family changed my life? Well my best friend has had the biggest influence on my life." Through the "So What?" skill lesson, Richard began to "make a case" to the college admissions panel. After the lesson, he focused on the role his girlfriend has played in helping him further his education:

> She has helped me and pushed me in school. She has encouraged me to do things I thought I couldn't do. She has done what my family has failed to do, which is to encourage me to continue my education. She made me take high level classes and set goals and accomplish them.

Gabriela's and Richard's essays are excellent examples of how students used the "So What?" skill lesson to focus their essays and share the ways their life experiences have had an impact on their personal character. The skill lesson on writing your "So What?" gave students an opportunity to step outside of their experience and reflect on why it not only mattered to them, but why it could matter for a broader audience. This was a challenging step for many of the students in the class. Both Sarah and Dan pointed out that their students often struggled to articulate in their writing the way personal experience has shaped them or, as Sarah stated in a conversation, "to share in their writing how what they have learned in the past has changed them in some way and propelled them forward." This reflective step was challenging because it required them to slow down, reflect, and make sense of their stories for a real audience.

Concluding the Essay. Along with teaching students how to make this move in their essays as a way of showing the lessons they have learned, as well as the attributes and beliefs they have to offer a college or university, the research and teaching team also provided further tips for ways to successfully conclude their essays, including:

a. expand upon the broader implications of your essay topic
b. consider linking your conclusion to your introduction and reiterating introductory phrases to establish balance
c. redefine a term used previously in your body paragraphs
d. frame your topic within a larger context or show that your topic has a widespread appeal
e. avoid summarizing the body paragraphs
f. leave readers with a strong impression.

Akeelah chose to write her essay about the birth of her younger sister, who has Down syndrome. In her initial draft, Akeelah described the birth of her younger sister and her initial excitement about having a new sister as a playmate:

> She was finally here! My six-year old self has been waiting nine long months for the sister I never had. I have a younger brother, which is great except he's a boy and he and I share the same birthday with two years in between us. A sister is something different, she's someone you can relate to and share everything with, and I was ready.

She went on in the essay to share her surprise when she learned her sister was sick. In her initial draft, Akeelah ended the essay by stating that her new baby sister was born with Down Syndrome and that this surprised her. After taking part in the "So What?" skill lesson, Akeelah centered her final essay on the birth of her younger sister, but she incorporated a "So What?" into the concluding paragraph to share what she has learned from this relationship:

> My youngest sister has Down Syndrome. She was born with fluid in her heart and lungs and she survived the unimaginable. I cannot even think of what life would be without her. She may have a mental disability, but she could fool anyone. Against the odds, she has taught me the power of self-confidence, truth, and an overall love of life. I've heard people say that the developmentally disabled are sad stories for people, but I think they might be the most beautiful inhabitants of this planet. My sister holds no grudges, is carefree, and loves life unconditionally. Without Alenah, I never would have understood anything about people with special needs and I would not have the same goals I have today. I hope to one day become a teacher who works with individuals with special needs, like my sister, so I can make a difference in their lives. I am grateful to know and understand another world is so pure and joyful that I could have never encountered without Alenah.

Before the skill lesson, Akeelah's essay shared a powerful narrative revealing her love and acceptance for her sister; however, it ended without giving the reader insight into how she had changed as a result of this relationship or how the relationship had shaped her future goals and aspirations. In the revised version, she makes the shift from a personal narrative to making a case for why her story adds value to a college or university and to our society. This is an example of a move young writers need to practice to write successful college admission essays.

CONCLUDING THE WORKSHOP

Writing samples are embedded throughout this chapter as a way of exhibiting the growth that took place in students' writing at different stages of the college admission essay workshop. Juana is just one student whose writing improved dramatically from her initial essay to her final. Her first draft, in which she reflected on a powerful life event, lacked a clear message and was only a paragraph in length:

> One life experience I have learned from was when I lived with my dad. He lowered my self-esteem and confidence. Whenever I tried to please him, he found a way to get mad. He never made an attempt to build a father-daughter relationship. Everything about me seemed to disappoint him. He always had something rude to say or he would order me around. If I didn't do what he wanted a bigger conflict would build. We never had time to be a real family.

Because of her growth as a writer and her desire to understand this real world, gate-opening genre, Juana was able to write a strong final essay. Rather than focus on a general description of her relationship with her father, she focused on a specific life event that taught her lessons about life and about her personal character. Juana's essay is one example of the impact this workshop had on students and their writing. Her final essay illustrates the important stories students chose to write about and the ways in which they incorporated the knowledge gained from the skill lessons into their college admission essays.

> When I was younger I remember my dad as being an alright dad. He wasn't the best, but he wasn't the worst. He would take us to the park and buy us ice cream. We always had a lot of fun. But then as I started growing up I noticed that he was always in a bad mood. He would see us playing in our yard and say "instead of being here messing around go clean or help your mom." We would do as we were told but be very unhappy. He could never ask us nicely. He always had to scream or yell at us. My dad had a party supply business and my sister and I helped him every weekend.

When customers asked if we were his daughters he would say, "No, they're just people that get in the way." He was ashamed of us. My sister and I felt so humiliated. We would not talk to him, which he always thought was funny. I would cry on our way home from the store because I felt like he hated me. He always found a way to hurt my feelings.

One day my younger sister, Sarah, bought my little sister a gray hamster named Dody. My dad was home that day and saw the hamster and started yelling. "Why didn't you guys tell me you were buying a hamster? We already have enough pets! We need to make decisions together!" My dad was yelling at my mom about having a hamster as a pet. "Mario, let's go to the room and talk this out," my mom told him. My sister and I were playing with the hamster when we heard a noise in the other room that sounded like someone had been slapped. We heard my mom yell, "Don't hit me!" and my sister, Sarah, ran to my mom's room. I couldn't believe my dad had slapped my mom. He had never done anything like that before and it was then I knew his anger was serious. My sister called the police. But when they arrived at our front door my mom didn't tell them the truth. She was too afraid. We all lived in fear of my dad.

The following week, my sister and I had had enough. We decided to move to our aunt's house. The next day my mom and little sisters followed in our footsteps. It felt surreal not having my dad breathe down our necks waiting to yell at us. That day was the worst and best day of my life. We could finally act like the kids we were and we didn't have to worry about getting in trouble. It felt like freedom.

There are days when I wonder why I have the unlucky fortune to end up with a cruel dad. But, I always remember my grandma's saying, "God only gives you as much as you can handle." Her words remind me to believe in myself and to remember I will always have the strength to handle life's challenges.

Juana's writing helps to illustrate the kinds of positive changes that took place in students' pieces. After taking part in the skill lessons, her message, length, and word choice improved and moved closer to fitting the genre expectations of a college admission audience. Her final introduction grabs the reader's attention by diving right into a description of her father's anger. The essay incorporates detail and dialogue to paint a picture of who her father is and how his mood swings impacted her. Juana's conclusion shares a lesson learned and suggests how the tumultuous relationship with her father has molded her into a strong and resilient young woman. Her writing growth in this essay helps illustrate the power of embedding this kind of real world, gate-opening writing workshop into the secondary curriculum.

EXTENSION ACTIVITIES AND PROFESSIONAL RESOURCES

One of the underlying goals of the college admission essay genre and an outcome of our work at Libertad is improving access to college, particularly for student populations who have been historically denied opportunities to gain admission and pursue higher education. Ultimately, this means identifying, developing, and including other workshops in the curriculum that integrate instruction on the details of the college application and admission process. However, it also is important to reinforce the learning that has taken place in the workshop via extension activities. A few possible activities include:

a. taking a field trip to a local college so students can tour dorms, classrooms, and libraries and meet with college admission counselors
b. showing students how to search for colleges and their admission requirements on the Internet, as well as providing a tutorial on how to complete the Free Application for Federal Student Aid (FAFSA)
c. offering guidance on responding to scholarship essay prompts and on applying to different colleges, especially those with daunting application packets
d. connecting with teachers and faculty in other disciplines and bringing them into the workshop (e.g., school counselors who can offer hands-on workshops to help students find the college that is a "perfect" fit or technology/computer teachers who can show students how to search for college scholarships online)
e. providing additional time in the computer lab so students may fine-tune their admission essays and essays for scholarship applications
f. invite admission officers from local colleges and universities to speak to students about their expectationsinvite students from local colleges and universities to talk about the college admission process and college life.

Teachers may extend their thinking and learning about the college admission essay genre by exploring professional resources. The following resources, which are cited throughout this book, may be used as a starting point to understanding some of the genre's purpose and audience:

a. Harry Bauld's (2005) *On Writing the College Application Essay: Secrets of a Former Ivy League Admissions Officer*
b. Edward B. Fiske and Bruce G. Hammond's (2009) *Fiske Real World College Essays That Work*
c. Alan Gelb's (2008) *Conquering the College Admissions Essay in 10 Steps: Crafting a Winning Personal Statement*
d. The Harvard Crimson's (2010) *50 Successful Harvard Application Essays: What Worked for Them Can Help You Get into the College of Your Choice* (3rd ed.)
e. Sarah Myers McGinty's (2006) *The College Application Essay* (Rev. ed.).

Although these resources helped the research and teaching team gain insight into some of the perceived expectations of college admissions panels, it is important to note that only one of these texts (Bauld, 2006) was written by an actual college admission officer. Although these guidebooks include helpful suggestions, they should not be used as a template or recipe for writing the college admission essay, especially for teachers working with ethnically and linguistically diverse student populations who are not well represented in the essay examples included in the books.

SUMMING UP

Because real world, gate-opening writing is tied to real contexts and audiences, it provides rich opportunities for students to learn about academic, professional, and civic activities that they may have never experienced in their young lives. By embedding real world, gate-opening writing into the secondary curriculum, teachers may do much more than just teach the skills and strategies associated with particular writing forms. They may provide instruction and opportunity for students to read, research, engage with, and reflect upon the contexts where writing takes place. The college admission essay is one kind of writing that is a part of a larger, real world context—the college application process.

If the goal of secondary English teachers is to open the doors of access for all students, then demystifying the many facets of the college admission process—including researching colleges and universities that make a good "fit" for students, filling out financial aid forms, taking the PSAT and SAT exams, applying for scholarships and student loans, taking college preparatory courses in high school, seeking letters of reference, and applying early decision—is worthy of time and attention. It is important to connect and build upon instructional units and to expand the curriculum beyond single tasks, such as writing the college admission essay, into broader themes that students can relate to and benefit from.

This workshop gave the research and teaching team an opportunity to understand the importance of exposing students to powerful writing genres like the college admission essay. It not only is a useful kind of writing, but it also signals to students the importance of learning about academic and professional writing that can open the gates of access to a world beyond high school. This workshop did not give all students perfect writing skills and access to higher education. In fact, as described in the next chapter, many aspects of the teaching and research of this curriculum were challenging and nuanced. Our teaching and research were continually influenced by the real world complexities of working in a school. If educators want to shake up the imbalances and inequities in schools, then we must be willing to take on challenging research and teaching projects, like this one, to ensure that students are exposed to the kinds of writing that have a real impact on their success in college, the workplace, and beyond.

CHAPTER 5

Using Points of Tension as Turning Points

From this workshop I learned not to be afraid or embarrassed to write about my life. I discovered that writing opens a door to the reader and, in a way, we let them into our lives by sharing our stories.

—Gladys, 12th-grade student, written reflection

After spending several weeks at Libertad High School, the research and teaching team came away feeling exhilarated by the connections with students and teachers and proud of the growth in students' writing. This chapter moves away from a wide-angle picture of the happenings related to the curriculum and shifts the lens to focus on points of tension and opportunities that arose from these challenges during the weeks at Libertad. This chapter also examines roadblocks students faced after the workshop despite the overall success of the workshop, and ways the research and teaching team tried to address these. As writing researchers and teachers, these moments brought about the greatest insight into what it is like to implement real world, gate-opening writing tasks in a classroom with ethnically and linguistically diverse students, many of whom are the first in their family to graduate high school and go to college, are facing challenging economic circumstances, and are learning English as a second language. This chapter explores self-efficacy and reflection, as well as the role they played, in this writing workshop. The chapter concludes by sharing lingering questions about ways this workshop could be extended and improved upon in other classrooms and in future studies.

SHIFTING PRACTICES TO SUPPORT LEARNING

In the weeks prior to the workshop at Libertad, the research and teaching team was challenged to look closely at the classrooms and at the perspectives of various social, cultural, and ideological contexts in the school and community. The research team began to take on an emic, or insider, view (Creswell, 1998; Spradley, 1979) of the world through the eyes of the teachers and students. The research team built ties with the classroom teachers, school administrators, and staff; spent time observing the classes before the start of the workshop, informally interviewing teachers and colleagues who had insight into the workings of the school and its community; and collected data on students' previous writing experiences. And even though the research team had taken time to learn about the school culture and gather information about students as individual learners, there were several points throughout the workshop where we needed to step back to reflect critically on what was taking place.

One of the most important turning points occurred in the first few days of the workshop when the research and teaching team encountered unexpected resistance from a few students. The teachers, Sarah and Dan, noticed that there were more behavior problems and disruptions than usual. For example, Cody continually tapped his pencil loudly and hummed. He was in good spirits but often cracked jokes and tested the situation. He refused to write.

Other students did not overtly disrupt the class like Cody did, but their inactivity signaled disengagement with the workshop. They sat quietly and politely, but they did not:

a. write more than a few words in an entire workshop session
b. take notes during skill lessons
c. share writing or personal details in class discussions
d. ask questions.

Although the majority of the students in both classes were participating, the disruptions and lack of involvement from some students were disheartening and set an uncomfortable tone for the research and teaching team as well as for other students involved at the onset of the workshop. The research and teaching team worried that these few students were communicating, in their own unique ways, that the workshop was not working for them. They were pushing back, and we wanted to understand why.

Although the workshop had just started, the research and teaching team had arrived at a crossroads. We realized that if we plowed forward without working through this point of tension, then we would be defeating every goal we had set for the research and workshop. Therefore, the research and teaching team met to talk about ways of building trust and creating a comfortable learning community. We discussed the complexity behind the resistance we were experiencing as researchers and teachers. First, as researchers, we acknowledged that even though we had spent time in the classroom observing, we were now acting in new roles as authorities and it would take some time to build a positive learning space and gain trust with the students.

Next, as teachers, we recognized that asking students to take part in a real world writing workshop to prepare a high-stakes essay meant asking them to think about, prepare for, and potentially impact their futures. The classroom teachers shared that many students were frightened about their next steps after high school and the college admission essay added to their anxiety.

The research and teaching team also reconsidered ways of using the corpus of college admission essays gathered prior to the essay. The research and teaching team had initially planned to weave selections and entire pieces from the sample essays into all of our skill lessons as mentor texts. We discussed the complexity of using mentor texts to give students examples of successful college admission essays and recognized that the mentor texts we had collected from college students around the country could be unintentionally shutting students down rather than supporting their writing. Many of the stories and experiences in the example essays came from students from different socioeconomic, geographic, ethnic, and linguistic backgrounds than the students at Libertad.

Finally, the research and teaching team acknowledged the ways we were reacting to the content in students' initial essays and how our first reactions, although unintentional, could shut students down rather than energize them to write. The research and teaching team learned from the very beginning of the workshop that points of tension like these could be used as turning points to improve the kinds of instruction taking place in the classroom. A window into a few of these points of tension and the ways the research and teaching team shifted practices to better support student learning is offered below.

Building a Positive Learning Space

As mentioned previously, a few students expressed disinterest in or resistance to the workshop in the beginning and, as a result, they were acting out or not responding to the curriculum. To address this issue, the research and teaching team implemented a number of strategies to foster a safe learning space and a better sense of community in the classroom. The research and teaching team originally had planned to have Sarah and Dan deliver the majority of the instruction because we had assumed this would cause the least disruption and provide teachers with ownership of the workshop curriculum. In the first days of the workshop, Sarah and Dan had distributed questionnaires, introduced the first skill lesson, conducted the workshops, and served as the main guides or coaches in the classroom. The other members of our research team either sat in desks in the back of the class or floated around the room to answer students' questions. As the research and teaching team reflected on this initial teaching decision, Sarah and Dan made the point that students were aware that the workshop was something new and exciting and the new faces, materials, and approaches to learning represented a shift in students' routine. However, Sarah and Dan could also see that it was confusing and frustrating for students not to have direct contact with the research team. Because of this, we decided to change our plans about who would deliver instruction from there on out.

Sarah and Dan felt students would respond better to the workshop if they received the majority of their instruction and direction from Arturo and Cynthia, the culturally and linguistically diverse doctoral students who were members of our research team, along with Jessica, rather than from their "normal" classroom teachers. This was a unique opportunity for students to receive instruction from individuals who shared similar cultural and linguistic backgrounds as well as from a professor connected to the local university that many of the students hoped to attend.

Respecting and Responding to Students' Fears

Another way the research and teaching team chose to address the resistance from students in the first days of the workshop was by acknowledging the fears students associated with applying and going to college. The research and teaching team did this by devoting half of one workshop to answering students' questions about the college admission essay and the admission process. This allowed students to express their fears and us to acknowledge them. Some students expressed how they wanted to go to college but were worried they would not have the money to pay for tuition. Others did not know if they could balance their studies with full-time jobs and family responsibilities. Undocumented students were concerned that their status would get in the way of their chance to receive a post-secondary education. When this workshop took place, several recently proposed state laws threatened many of the students and their parents. For example, State of Arizona House Bill 2281 (2010) bans classes aimed at or are offered for certain ethnic groups. It has also outlawed classes that advocate overthrow of the U.S. government, promote resentment toward a race or class or people, or advocate ethnic solidarity. Additionally, the state's controversial anti-immigration bill, "Support Our Law Enforcement and Safe Neighborhoods Act," State of Arizona Senate Bill 1070 (2010), sparked a national debate about the civil rights of individuals, particularly the children of undocumented immigrants who attend public schools. These policies helped give rise to a politically charged atmosphere in the state and in local schools, causing many students to be uneasy about their educational futures.

Because the college admission essay is a real world, gate-opening genre with consequences attached, it made sense that students had concerns about this writing task. It was necessary to acknowledge and respond to students' anxieties before moving forward with the writing workshop. To help address these issues, over the course of the workshop, the undergraduate research assistant, Sara, created and provided pamphlets describing undergraduate scholarships offered through the state university system and examples of financial aid packages. She also invited, organized, and participated in a multiethnic panel of undergraduates from the local university to come to class one day to address students' questions about the application process and about attending college. The research and teaching team hoped to alleviate some of the fear so students could home in on the writing task at hand. Another way we worked to alleviate students' anxiety regarding the college admission essay workshop was to reconsider the use of college admission essay samples we had collected from college students and guidebooks.

Rethinking Mentor Texts

A mentor text exemplifies a genre and serves as an example for writers who are in similar situations or contexts as the mentor text author (Charney & Carlson, 1995; Robb, 2010). Teachers may present mentor, or model, texts to students as a way of providing insight into how to compose a particular piece of writing. Before the workshop, as noted in the previous chapter, Jessica and Sara, the undergraduate research assistant, compiled a set of 50 model admission essays, which they then read and analyzed. Jessica and Meredith also read and analyzed five college admission essay guidebooks produced by former admissions officers, universities, and testing corporations (see Bauld, 2005; Fiske & Hammond, 2009; Gelb, 2008; The Harvard Crimson, 2010; McGinty, 2006) as a way to become familiar with the college admission essay genre. After reading examples from the guidebooks and the students' essays closely and taking part in conversations as a research and teaching team, the research and teaching team decided that many of the essay topics from the model essays were not a good match for the students in our workshop. That is, the topics reflected the fact that most of the students who wrote the model essays came from dramatically different social, cultural, and educational backgrounds than the students in the workshop.

Initially, the essays and guidebooks were collected to provide examples of successful college admission essays. The research and teaching team thought that if we learned more about the genre, then this knowledge might transfer to the students. At that time, the research and teaching team thought of this form of writing as just that: a form to analyze, break into steps, and demystify for students. Although this remained one of our main goals throughout the writing workshop, the research and teaching team also came to realize that this written genre cannot be understood merely as a set of features put together in a certain way to make a successful text. It was important to remember that, although written for a distant or academic audience, the college admission essay is a personal statement that is deeply connected to students' social, cultural, and educational experiences.

Through the process of collecting and analyzing model essays, the research and teaching team came to realize that most represented the financial, educational, and racial privilege of dominant culture in the United States. The research and teaching team worried that the subject matter would not support students who came from divergent lived experiences. For example, many of the model essays explored students' access to costly educational experiences such as studying abroad in countries like France, Great Britain, and Israel and to costly extracurricular activities like an out-of-town astronomy camp, sailboat racing, and mission trips to Guatemala, Bolivia, and Nicaragua. As some of the guidebooks mention, diversity is valued in college admission essays, yet of the 50 students who wrote the essays Jessica and Sara had collected, 42 openly acknowledge in their writing that they come from stable, privileged environments, not environments riddled by economic poverty. Three essays discussed the economic and social challenges death and illness can cause. Further, while five essays explored racial and ethnic identity or cultural duality, only one discussed what it was like to live in an urban community and none of the essays discussed what it was like to be a Mexican American immigrant learning to speak English and attempting to acclimate to culture in the United States, an experience several of the students in the workshop were going through and ultimately chose to write about in their essays.

The following excerpt, written by a 12th-grade high school male who attended a prestigious private school in the same city as Libertad, represents the kind of writing Jessica and Sara had initially collected:

> I spent my junior year of high school living with a host family in Japan. I attended a Japanese high school and took Japanese classes. At first, my elementary level of Japanese was clearly inadequate to even be productive in the classes and assimilation

> seemed a daunting undertaking. I learned five words a day every three months and things started to pull together and make sense. I could finally talk to my teachers and classmates. Beyond my still floundering grammar, I had much more to learn, not about the language, but about the culture. The vast differences between my culture and Japanese culture seemed to be widening. Upon my return, I realized that because I had grown used to Japan, now America seemed odd and quirky. I have had many unusual experiences, not just from Japan, but everywhere else my traveling-obsessed family has taken me. I have been diving in Fiji, bungee jumping in Thailand, and canoeing in Panama. This list is long, just as my global awareness and sense of diversity is large. I believe, although I am a Caucasian American, I bring the diversity of the globe and the perspectives of the people in it.

After reading through sample essays like this, the research and teaching team realized many of these "mentor" texts might not serve as mentors at all. Jessica also found that the majority of the examples provided in our collection of college admission guidebooks reflected similar stories of economic security and privilege. For example, in Fiske and Hammond's (2009) *Real College Essays that Work*, the authors share 109 essays from students around the country. However, Jessica only found 11 essays that shared stories of ethnicity, language, or poverty. McGinty's (2006) *The College Application Essay* includes wonderful tips to help students craft college admission essays along with 12 sample essays to serve as mentor texts. However, only one of the sample essays describes the experience of a first-generation immigrant student who grew up in poverty and all of the other examples portray lived experiences that diverge greatly from those of the students taking part in the workshop. The research and teaching team worried that many of these model essays might have the reverse effect and unintentionally disenfranchise students rather than invite them into the writing process. This was not because the students in the workshop were without compelling life experiences. In fact, the students at Libertad had remarkable stories to tell. However, their stories reflected their unique social, cultural, linguistic, and familial histories, ones that are not often privileged in institutions of power or, it turns out, in guidebooks on writing college admission essays. The research and teaching team realized, though, that if we wanted to open the gates of the college admission essay to students, we shouldn't further highlight the privileges that many students in the workshop did not have access to. Rather than using complete sample essays, the research and teaching team opted to use excerpts from these essays that represented specific writing choices, or genre features for specific skill lessons. In future workshops, we hope to include the corpus of essays collected from students at Libertad as mentor texts along with essays from guidebooks and other successful essays from college students across the country. The research and teaching team's decision to reevaluate the use of mentor texts at Libertad was just one of the many strategic and reflective moves made while conducting the workshop.

Honoring Students' Topic Choices

Within the first few days of the writing workshop, as students began drafting their initial essays, the research and teaching team conferred with them about their topic choices and immediately noticed almost all were writing about deeply personal and self-revelatory subject matter (e.g., overcoming traumatic hardship such as illness, injury, or death). After the first read through of students' essays, the research and teaching team felt conflicted about the topics as a whole and worried that students should write more "traditional" essays for a college admissions audience—essays about personal achievements, inspirational and uplifting mentors, or positive life experiences.

Although it is difficult to admit now, the research and teaching team first reacted to the topic choices by saying things like, "This is an important story to tell, but a college admission committee may prefer you tell a story that is not so painful or personal." The research and teaching team began to notice, however, that this feedback caused many students to immediately shut down or stop writing. In defense, Talia said, "If I don't write about this experience, then I don't have anything to write about at all. This is what happened to me that matters the most, and I don't have anything else to share that matters as much." When the research and teaching team told students that their stories were not a good fit for the college admission essay, we were, in effect, telling them that their lived experience would not be valued or appreciated by a powerful and, in their eyes, wise audience. What we thought was going to help students become successful with this genre and get into college was actually an affront to their lives and stories.

After one class of discouraging exchanges with students, we called a research and teaching team meeting to discuss our unsettling reactions to the students' essay topics. We all were uncomfortable telling students that their stories were not valuable for this genre, but we wanted to examine why we were feeling this way and unintentionally communicating this message about their topics and what we could do to better support students in their writing. After much reflection and discussion, the research and teaching team realized we had preconceived notions of what counted as an appropriate or valued topic choice for this genre. We had made assumptions about the kinds of topics we thought students would choose based upon our:

a. personal experiences, social class, and cultural backgrounds
b. samples of successful college admission essays we had collected and analyzed prior to the study
c. review of college admission essay guidebooks and websites produced by former admissions officers, universities, and testing corporations.

The research and teaching team knew the students we were working with came from low-income families and many were recent immigrants living in a high-poverty community. It was no surprise to us nor was it a novelty to find that a great many of the students had suffered a degree of hardship in their young lives. However, we were so invested in trying to "successfully" teach the college admission essay genre and we had become so immersed in finding mentor texts through the guidebooks and sample essays we had collected to prepare our lessons and teaching plans that we had lost sight, to some degree, of the individuals sitting in front of us. As noted previously, most of the sample essays the research team had collected prior to the workshop had been written by students who came from dramatically different social, cultural, and educational backgrounds than the students participating in our workshop. The research and teaching team realized we were projecting the values and beliefs of the dominant culture, as well as our own experiences with this writing task, onto students' personal stories rather than honoring the stories and students' lived experiences.

As we reflected upon students' topics, we also realized we felt a sense of urgency surrounding the genre. Risk is involved when students write for real audiences, especially when these audiences may use the writing samples to grant or deny entrance into institutions of power, like colleges and universities. The research and teaching team knew students were going to use these essays to apply for colleges as well as scholarships, so we wanted them to "get the essays right." However, as we grappled with whether to have students pursue different topics, the research and teaching team came to understand that it was not our place to tell students what topics counted for this genre or would be considered "correct." We were reminded that the teaching of real world and gate-opening writing is a dialogic, or two-way, communication process. On the one hand, writing teachers work to actively demystify genres for their students by teaching the expectations of the genre, sharing model texts, and deconstructing "moves" writers make in creating successful texts. At the same time, students in any writing class bring their unique experiences, cultures, languages, and lenses to every piece of writing regardless of genre. The students in this study were drawing on powerful "aspirational, social, navigational, linguistic, resistant and familial capital" (Yosso, 2005, p. 69). The research and teaching team ultimately concluded that these forms of cultural capital deserve a place in the secondary classroom and in colleges and universities, regardless of whether these stories have traditionally been deemed significant for this genre by academia and other institutions of power.

The research and teaching team returned to the teaching of the writing workshop and told students to write their essays about the stories and topics that mattered to them and explained that our initial reaction had been a misstep. The research and teaching team also chose to focus instruction on teaching skills and strategies to demystify the key genre elements of the college admission essay. For example, we addressed audience awareness when selecting a topic by helping students envision who they might be writing for and why, but felt that it was not our job to dictate what topics were appropriate. In fact, the research and teaching team chose to celebrate students' stories by sharing portions of their essays aloud during the writing process in pair, group, and whole-class settings.

Once the research and teaching team became more aware of our own discomfort, preconceived notions, and personal subjectivities (Peshkin, 1988), we realized that having so many students write about deeply personal and self-revelatory experiences was a key finding in our workshop that we wanted to examine further. As researchers and teachers, our decision to honor students' lived experiences through their topic choices, rather than fixating on what we thought students were supposed to write or achieve with their essays, helped us rethink what counted as a successful college admission essay and opened up the possibilities for this genre and for our analysis of student writing. The research and teaching team also realized that one of the main reasons we were experiencing some resistance to the workshop was connected to the way students viewed themselves as writers. Allowing students to write about the topics that mattered to them was not only a way to honor their lived experience, but also helped build their confidence about writing in general.

BUILDING WRITING CONFIDENCE

As noted previously, a primary goal for the workshop was to increase students' confidence and knowledge about a real world, gate-opening

TABLE 5.1. Writing Self-Efficacy Scores
(Class A & B Sample Scores Pre- and Post-Workshop)

	Pre	Post
Overall Understanding of the College Admission Essay	4.5	8
Understanding Elements of a College Admission Essay	4.6	7.9
Writing an Introduction for the College Admission Essay	5.5	8.1
Writing a Conclusion for the College Admission Essay	6.1	7.9
Understanding the College Admission Essay Audience	5	7.5
Understanding of the College Admission Process	5	7.6

Note. Scores are based on a scale of 0 to 10 ("0" representing "not confident at all" and 10 representing "very confident").

writing task. Research on self-efficacy or self-confidence has shown that people's beliefs about the world and how they are situated in it allows them to have some control over their actions, decisions, and feelings (Bandura, 1986). The concept of self-efficacy can also be extended to classroom writing because students' interpretations about their potential to achieve academic success are integral to their success as writers (Pajares, 2003). For example, if students believe they are strong writers, then they are more likely to react positively to challenging writing tasks such as the college admission essay. Research consistently shows that students' self-confidence is related to writing performance (Graham & Harris, 2005; Pajares & Johnson, 1994; Pajares, Johnson, & Usher, 2007; Zimmerman & Bandura, 1994).

However, research also shows that writing self-efficacy levels often drop in middle school and remain at that level through high school (Usher & Pajares, 2008). This is especially a concern for English language learners and low-income, multiethnic youth who attend "underperforming" secondary schools and are routinely sorted into remedial English courses where writing instruction often centers around test preparation for improving scores on state-mandated exams (Applebee & Langer, 2009; Kohn, 1999). Over time, there is a risk that students in these lower-level courses may lose confidence in their academic abilities or view writing and reading as punitive tasks that are disconnected from their lives rather than skills that can help them plan for their future.

Jessica realized early in the workshop how important it would be to learn more about how this instructional unit had an impact on students' self-confidence with the college admission essay. She asked students to fill out pre- and post-workshop writing self-efficacy questionnaires (see Chapter 4), where they could rank their feelings associated with this type of writing, at the beginning and again at the end of the workshop.

At the beginning of the workshop, students on average rated their understanding of the college admission essay a 4.5 out of 10. This score signaled to the research and teaching team that the college admission essay was a genre that students needed more exposure to because students did not report feeling very confident with this kind of writing. The research and teaching team was pleased to know, though, that after the workshop the self-confidence scores showed great improvement. Students reported feeling more confident and knowledgeable about the college admission essay and, as a result, students' ratings improved from 4.5 to 8.0 out of 10 (see Table 5.1).

Beyond just collecting numbers that show the influence of this workshop on students' self-confidence with the college admission essay, the research and teaching team wanted to hear from the students directly about this workshop and how it influenced the way they felt about writing the college admission essay. To do this, Jessica asked students to respond to a post-workshop reflection she had created (see Appendix B). This included a series of questions asking students to describe their reactions to the workshop and feelings associated with writing the college admission essay. The research team also formally and informally interviewed four students and both classroom teachers 1 month after the completion of the workshop to gain a better sense of their feelings and beliefs toward this writing task and the workshop experience as a whole. These open-ended interviews included ten questions, which covered four categories: (1) reflection questions on the workshop as a whole, (2) future plans and goals, (3) obstacles to attending college, and (4) general feelings about writing. In response to a question about her future goals, Gladys shared her dream of becoming a professional woman who will help support a family:

> I've always wanted to go to college. I've always seen myself dressed in professional clothes. I want to wear a blazer to work. I just don't know what I want to be. I'm not sure. I just know I want to have a big house and support my family. I just don't have a clear picture of it yet.

Gladys also described how her mother has encouraged her to succeed in school and has served as an important sponsor for Gladys's academic achievement:

> My mom has always encouraged me to go on with school. She tells me she doesn't want me to be stuck like she is. She wants me to get settled in a job and then get married and have kids. I tell my siblings to work hard. I am going to be their example and graduate and I want them to follow in my path.

The post-workshop interviews were planned as a way to further contextualize how the college admission essay workshop fit into students' larger goals and aspirations regarding college. The research team hoped students would describe the range of emotions, attitudes, and beliefs that this workshop conjured. The majority of the students expressed great enthusiasm about the workshop and their newfound writing confidence. In her interview, Gloria explained, "I never thought my writing was good enough to get into college even though I have always gotten good grades. But now, I feel more confident." Jacqueline could not hide her growing belief in her writing when she shared the following in her interview with Jessica that took place after the completion of the workshop: "You guys made me feel confident about my writing and that I am able to go on in life to accomplish anything!" Raymundo noted the difference in his confidence before and after the workshop in an interview: "I feel more comfortable in my writing abilities—much better than how I felt before the workshop." In the post-workshop reflections and interviews, students expressed more confidence with this gate-opening genre and some even suggested that they were more confident with the overall college application process after the workshop. Students generally expressed an overall increase in confidence associated with the college admission essay and the college application process. This highlights the importance of giving students the opportunity to experience different kinds of real world, gate-opening writing that they had not been exposed to before the workshop.

THE POWER OF ACCESS

The college admission essay workshop was about far more than deconstructing key ingredients that make up a successful college admission essay. This workshop was also about demystifying the college admission audience and application process and building confidence in a group of adolescent writers who began the workshop feeling anxious. Dan described how this workshop represented a shift for his students in the way they thought about themselves as writers and as prospective college students:

> Sometimes when you think your writing isn't very good, which is the way many of my students feel, and especially when you are writing a college admission essay with high stakes attached, it almost makes students feel like they aren't very good. Helping my students understand this kind of writing and make their essays better has helped them in their view of themselves as individuals, as college-bound students.

The workshop gave students an opportunity to see that writing a college admission essay was something they could successfully accomplish despite perceived limitations. In her post-workshop interview, Abril said, "Even though it seemed like a difficult and scary task, this workshop showed me that writing a college admission essay is actually not that hard. It helps knowing that the essay should be about my own thoughts and feelings and experiences instead of just an explanation of my transcripts." She also noted the way the workshop gave her access to the genre expectations.

Abril was not alone in thinking prior to the workshop that the college admission essay should be a list of her accomplishments or a retelling of her resume. Once she realized she could tell a story in her essay about an important event or an experience with an important mentor, she felt more at ease as a writer. Abril felt the workshop gave her confidence to believe in her own story and lived experiences and to share these with a college admissions audience.

In his post-workshop interview, Ernesto reflected on the gate-opening aspects of the admission essay and the importance of making a positive impact on college admission officers: "I hadn't realized until now that this essay is a chance for the college to get to know me. It will be the first impression I make on them." Ernesto explained that this shift in his thinking after participating in the skill lesson on audience awareness helped alleviate some of his fear about writing the essay in the first place. "Once I realized this was an opportunity for people to get to know me, instead of a required way for them to judge me, then I could breathe easier and write."

Many of the students also found certain lessons associated with key genre elements and elements of the writing process helpful. Students described the pre-writing, introductory writing, and conclusion skill lessons as particularly beneficial. Cody reported in his post-workshop reflection, "I learned that it helps me to use webs to brainstorm my ideas before I begin writing," whereas Jazmine stated in her interview, "I learned how to put together my essay rather than just writing. I also learned how to include description and how to end strongly." Similarly, Ramiro wrote in his post-workshop reflection, "I learned to open up to my audience in a new way and how to grab my reader's attention and keep them entertained. I also learned how to finish with a strong conclusion—a clincher." Mariah said:

> I learned that I need to include many different writing strategies in my essay and to tell my story instead of just sharing information about myself. I also learned to put my heart into my writing and make the reader know about myself so my writing will stand out.

Ernesto wrote, "I learned how to expose myself to the reader and how to share my point of view even though my audience may think differently than I do."

Much to the surprise of the research and teaching team, some students expressed how the workshop prepared them for real world, gate-opening writing tasks beyond the essay and helped them feel more capable and confident as soon-to-be college writers. In an interview with Arturo, Gladys shared how the workshop prepared her to apply for scholarships and to apply for admission to a range of colleges and universities:

> On Friday, I found out during my first-period class that there was a scholarship due. My friend was freaking out about all of the requirements, but I already had what I needed from this workshop. My essay topic fit the scholarship prompt perfectly and I felt like I had already received help on everything that I needed. I hear a lot of my friends tell me they are not going to apply for scholarships or opportunities because of the personal statement. I already have this. I applied to Arizona State University, Northern Arizona University, and Colorado State University. I got accepted to one and I'm waiting to hear about the others.

The teachers' feedback about the workshop also reinforced students' sentiments. Dan commented on his students' improved writing skills and increased confidence. He explained,

> I think my students really expressed their experiences well in their essays. Every student who participated in the 2008 workshop at Libertad High School was accepted to a post-secondary institution. All the students applied to at least one 4-year college or university, and the majority used the essays generated in our workshop to apply for scholarships.

As Sarah explained, "I was thrilled to have all of my students apply to colleges. This has been a goal of mine for years as a teacher working with seniors in high school, and it means a lot to see students taking steps to pursue next steps in their schooling." Dan was equally enthusiastic and explained,

> Many students ended up using their college admission essays to apply for scholarships and a number of them actually won based on their essays. It turned into a positive cycle. Once a few students found out they had won, then everybody started to get excited.

The workshop gave students access to information, skills, and practice to support them in preparing essays they could then use for college, university, and scholarship applications. Students who participated in the workshop all walked away with an essay they could use, if they chose, to pursue post-secondary opportunities that required this kind of writing sample. As Gladys mentioned above, when she heard about a scholarship opportunity that many of her friends were not applying for because it required a writing sample, she jumped on it because she had what she needed. The workshop gave students access to a piece of writing they need to open doors for their next life steps.

CONFRONTING ROADBLOCKS ABOUT ATTENDING COLLEGE

Despite the praise from students and teachers about what students gained from the workshop and despite the points of tension in the workshop we were able to overcome as a group, many students shared concerns about possible roadblocks along their path toward a post-secondary institution. As previously noted, many of the students were going to be the first in their family to graduate from high school and pursue higher education. Although the intention was to support students as writers working with an important real world, gate-opening genre, this study was not meant to be a simple how-to recipe for getting ethnically and linguistically diverse learners into college. But because the college admission essay opens doors and helps youth gain admission to important institutions, many students' reactions to the workshop fell well beyond the subject of writing and were connected to their questions, concerns, and anxieties about the realities of moving beyond high school and attending a 4-year college or university. For example, every student expressed some concern at the end of the workshop about the cost of college tuition. More than anything else, they felt finances could stand in their way of attending college. Many students stated they would have to work at least two jobs to pay tuition. Others said they would have to work for several months to save enough money to pay tuition. Victor, for example, told Arturo in his post-workshop interview that he was going to work for a while to save money, then attend classes at a local community college to accumulate credits at an affordable rate, and finally transfer to the major university in the area to earn his bachelor's degree. When Arturo mentioned some of the challenges this path might present, Victor said, "Don't worry. I'll do it. I can do it." These concerns were common and real for students.

A few students expressed anxiety about moving away from their families, and others shared how family obligations could make it difficult to "break away" and leave home. In her interview with Arturo after the workshop, Gladys expressed her reservations about leaving home:

> I have applied to four universities and I've already heard back from one telling me I was accepted. I'm really excited but just scared. I'm close with my family and my younger siblings and I don't want to live apart from them. Also, I can't drive. I don't even have my permit. I worry about transportation. I also worry because I don't know how to cook. Will I have to cook for myself?

Although Gladys was well on her path toward college, having received one acceptance notice from a local university and submitted scholarships and applications for a number of other schools, she was concerned about such a huge life change. Although hesitation and anxiety about college is normal for most high school seniors thinking about leaving home, Gladys wanted Arturo to know that her concerns felt overwhelming. "I'm just worried. . . . I don't want to end up feeling too scared and paralyzed to move forward with my life."

Students' concerns about attending college helped complicate our notions of what it means to prepare students for post-secondary schooling and to teach real world writing tasks. The research and teaching team were continually reminded of the ways real world, gate-opening writing tasks, like the college admission essay, are deeply intertwined with economic, social, and cultural ties. Through the workshop, students communicated how getting into and attending college is not as simple as writing a good essay or achieving a high SAT score. Students' economic and familial obligations were not simply speed bumps on their paths, but were tied to deeply held beliefs about their roles as young men and women and were representative of the struggles many youth of color are faced with in the United States. Victor shared in his post-workshop interview that his first priority is his responsibility to his family:

> Maybe I could get scholarships to help pay my tuition but if my dad gets hurt at work or my mom gets injured, I am going to have to step up and take care of my family. College will not be what comes first if this were to happen. It's my responsibility to be the provider as the oldest child. A lot of kids can plan for college without having this be the first thing on their minds. Not me. This is what I think about more than anything else.

In the same breath, Victor went on to explain that he was concerned about "some of the same things other students my age are worried about when it comes to applying for college." He really wanted to improve his low SAT scores. He said, "My SAT scores are a problem. I have to take that test again. I got a 980 the first time. That's really bad. Then, the second time, I got 940, which is worse. I have to take it again to try to do better." Even though Victor has complex concerns based on his family's socioeconomic status, he is still subject to the simple concerns of students of privilege.

Gladys's and Victor's anxieties were representative of the many complex obstacles that ethnically and linguistically diverse students faced in their path to college. It is imperative that secondary educators recognize the numerous and wide-ranging barriers students encounter as they transition to college. It is part of our many duties as educators to recognize and support students as they work to address and overcome these barriers and pursue their life goals.

LINGERING QUESTIONS

This curricular unit and research endeavor was not a panacea that eliminated students' fears, erased real and persistent roadblocks, or solved all writing challenges for this group of students. Nor was this workshop an easy or quick fix for getting low-income, ethnically and linguistically diverse youth into college. After the workshop, the research and teaching team were left with some roadblocks and lingering questions about ways to extend and improve this project.

First, we wondered whether the writing workshop had an impact on students' college application choices. As a research and teaching team, we did not know if students applied to certain colleges based upon their admission essay or if they were more likely to apply to college as a result of the workshop. Future workshops could expand this curriculum to include instruction on the college application and admission process and our workshop could also be enhanced by following students through their first year of college to trace the number who pursue post-secondary schooling.

Along with experiencing the rich rewards that come with teaching a diverse and lively group of adolescent writers, the research and teaching team also experienced some of the challenges that go along with teaching any group of students. The majority of the students completed a polished and "ready-to-use" college admission essay. In fact, most of the students used their essays when they applied for colleges, universities, and scholarships in the months following the workshop. However, there were a few students at the end of our time at Libertad who turned in essays that might be red flags for college admission officers. These essays were incomplete or not polished enough to submit to an admissions panel due to apparent language barriers or frequent absences caused by illness, scheduling conflicts, sports events, and family obligations.

Although the research and teaching team worked to honor students' native languages in the workshop, there were still some students who struggled with syntax, grammar, and general facility with language, and this, in the end, influenced the overall clarity and presentation of their final product. There were also a few essays that were incomplete or lacking in focus and were clearly a product of missed instructional time. A couple of students transferred into the classes after the first 2 weeks of the workshop. At the time the workshop was taking place, the high school counselors were in the process of rearranging students' schedules because the school was experiencing an extreme teacher shortage due to district budget cuts. As a result, students were shifted into new and larger classes and the research and teaching team experienced students transferring in and out of the workshop unexpectedly. Although we tried to support students who joined the class in the middle of the workshop by meeting with them before school and during lunch, providing them with copies of handouts and models they had missed from skill lessons, and checking in with them frequently to see that they received extra guidance and support, we also realized that it was impossible for these students to completely catch up after missing so much of the setup, instruction, and writing time.

After the completion of the workshop and analysis of the essays, Jessica and Meredith noticed that the essays written by students who missed more than one class session, particularly classes in the beginning of the workshop that were devoted to demystifying the genre, were lacking in clarity or were impersonal or incomplete. For example, Jon's final essay was only two paragraphs long and simply repeated that he has an optimistic personality. The piece felt like a free-write or first attempt rather than a final draft. As the research and teaching team read essays like Jon's, we were left wondering what we could have done differently to better support students who missed valuable instructional time.

SUMMING UP

Despite some of these challenges and lingering questions, the research and teaching team ended the workshop feeling confident that these students were better prepared to write college admission essays than they were before the workshop. Our hope is that with the help of their devoted classroom teachers, the lessons learned from the challenges they've overcome, and the support of their family and friends, students like Victor, Gladys, Akeelah, and Cody move on and become successful college writers.

The points of tension described in this chapter also suggest the need for teachers to monitor students' personal beliefs about specific writing tasks (Pajares et al., 2007). More specifically, ethnically and linguistically diverse students from underserved communities will benefit not only from gaining access to the writing skills and strategies necessary to succeed at writing real world, gate-opening genres like college admission essays but also from believing they are capable of succeeding at these important writing tasks (Hackett, 1995). Teachers may easily measure students' self-confidence associated with particular genres and writing tasks by incorporating reflections before and after instructional units (Hansen, 1998). The use of a real world, gate-opening writing curriculum with a focus on students' voices, strengths, and self-confidence about writing tasks in the classroom may be a successful tool to support ethnically and linguistically diverse students as they work toward post-secondary schooling. Even more, points of tension in the classroom may be used as reflective learning opportunities to turn the tides of the classroom and better meet students' needs. Taking these steps in writing curriculum and in the college admission process may help open more gates to college and beyond for diverse secondary writers.

CHAPTER 6

Drawing on Cultural Capital to Build Writing Capital

This workshop awakened my students to the power of writing for their present and future lives. Students walked away from this experience with powerful personal statements they could then turn around and use for applications and scholarships. Writing in this workshop became a way for students to reflect upon who they are as individuals and see the value in where they come from and where they're going.

—Dan, classroom teacher, interview

Dan describes the rich stories that emerged from the ethnically and linguistically diverse secondary writers who participated in the college admission essay workshop. Even after the workshop ended, Jessica and Meredith worked to gain further insight into students as writers and as individuals through a close analysis of their essays. To provide thick description in the narrative and to allow the reader to see a more complete picture of the participants (see Geertz, 1973), this chapter focuses on unveiling the topics and themes students wrote about, as well as what these suggest about working with ethnically and linguistically diverse writers. Before delving into these topics, however, it's important to detail the steps Jessica and Meredith took in the analysis and discovery of the themes that emerged from students' essays.

THEMES THAT EMERGED FROM OUR ANALYSIS

To understand and interpret the stories, experiences, and perspectives revealed in students' college admission essays, we applied grounded theory to develop themes inductively and to allow for multiple interpretations of the essays (see Strauss & Corbin, 1990). We analyzed the essays using a recursive process called the constant comparison method, which allows for each step of the data collection and analysis process to feed into the next and includes a process of revisiting and coding essays (for example, Patton, 1990).

In the first stage, we organized the essays by coding and "chunking" quotes according to similar patterns (see Early & Shagoury, 2010, and Sipe & Ghiso, 2004). "Chunking" refers to the process of pulling quotes from texts and organizing them based on key themes or categories. We coded each essay in our first run-through of the data without inference.

In the second stage, we made lists of codes to see if any of the codes from the first run through could be collapsed into a more reasonable number (see Marshall & Rossman, 1999). The process of collapsing codes resulted in a set of four themes. They are listed here in order of prominence:

a. overcoming hardship
b. extracurricular and academic support programs
c. cultural and ethnic identity
d. positive role of maternal figures.

In the third stage, we organized the four themes into more specific subcategories. For example, we organized "overcoming hardship" into two subcategories: "familial hardship" and "hardship caused by injury, illness, or death." We then determined which subcategories were robust or frequently appeared based on the number of essays per theme. If a subcategory had fewer than four essays, it was considered too narrow to be representative of the participants as a group and was then collapsed into a larger theme. For example, Antonio wrote about his hero, Batman. Initially, his essay was coded to fit a subcategory "popular culture," but after further analysis, we noticed this was the only essay that focused on popular culture. Because we wanted to value all students' topics and we wanted to make sense of all the essays, instead of discounting Antonio's topic choice or viewing it as an anomaly, we took part in another close reading of his essay to understand his use of popular culture. In this reading, we noticed how Antonio described Batman as a larger-than-life hero he looked up to. Antonio had struggled to speak English when he started 1st grade because he had recently immigrated to the United States and spoke Spanish only at home. Antonio admired Batman because he was so strong and outgoing and "devoted to helping people and learning new things." We noted that Antonio's essay did focus on a hero from popular culture, but we also recoded the essay to fit into the theme of cultural and ethnic identity.

Further, some of the essays overlapped and did not fit neatly into one category or another, so we chose to code these essays for more than one theme. This allowed us to interpret data in fresh ways and reframe our categories to be inclusive and to take into consideration different perspectives and viewpoints. For instance, one essay detailed Jenissa's relationship with her grandmother, her grandmother's death, and the hardships she overcame after losing her grandmother, the most important person in her life. We coded this essay under "overcoming hardship," more specifically "hardship caused by injury, illness, or death," as well as "maternal figures."

Along with the four main themes for the essay topics, we also found one theme that extended across the essays and was not connected to topic choice. We noted the importance of students calling upon their home or native languages. Making systematic decisions regarding our analysis of the essays allowed us to discover the most important themes and gave us a more nuanced picture of the students as individuals and writers.

Overcoming Hardship

Forty-eight percent of the essays told stories of resilience and persistence toward college despite challenging and traumatic life events. As noted, two subcategories emerged within the general theme of "overcoming hardship": 1) familial hardship and 2) hardship caused by injury, illness, or death.

Familial Hardship. Twenty-four percent of the students wrote essays that included stories of familial hardship such as limited economic resources, divorce, physical and emotional abuse, depression, and addiction. As we read the painful and self-revelatory material, we gained insight into the challenges students and their families face. For example, Cody's essay revealed a painful story of family drug abuse, as illustrated by the following excerpt:

> My family is not exactly the best group of people. However, they are the number one reason I plan to go to college. Other than my parents, my whole family is addicted to drugs. None of them have graduated from college. I have faced many issues with my family, and peer pressure is something they make me face every day. My family makes fun of me for being clean. They always try to convert me. I have stayed clean so I can finish college and go on to live a better life than anybody in my family. I am willing to work hard and risk everything for that dream. I want a better life.

Other students shared stories of either witnessing or experiencing physical and emotional abuse from family members. Jaime's essay focuses on his memories of feeling isolated and terrified when his mother and stepfather fought:

> It was a nightmare to listen to them fight. Some nights, I would just lie in my bed and cry to sleep. One day, all of the fighting reached a peak. My mom was planning a trip with my little brother, who was three at the time. My step father was giving my little brother a bath when she told him she had to take my brother on a trip. My step father told her she could not leave, but she tried to take my little brother out of the tub anyway. Then, my step father proceeded to hit her. I saw every punch hit her body from the hallway. I wanted to jump on him and make him stop, but my legs wouldn't carry me. All I could do was scream.

Ricardo shared memories of waiting for his father to return home from work while his depressed mother locked herself in her room day after day. Colby wrote about his feelings of alienation after painful life events, including his parents' divorce and the death of his sister, and at the recurring abuse at the hands of his stepfather. He learned to "bury my problems and hide my depression until I couldn't take the pain any longer." Colby started cutting himself and drinking to release and mask his pain. Along with all the hardship in his life, he also felt isolated and ostracized because of his Native American heritage and his sexual orientation.

Although essays like Jaime's, Akeelah's, and Colby's reveal vulnerable and self-revelatory subject matter, students' stories of familial hardship described how their traumatic life events had shaped their worldview and influenced their academic and life goals. For example, Colby ended his essay with a paragraph describing how he reached out to friends for support and started to work toward his future:

> I have learned to talk to my friends about who I am and how I am feeling and I have stopped hurting myself. I am striving to gain admission to college and I have kept myself busy as President of the Native American Club. My life has been full of hardship and heartbreaks that I want to leave in the dust. Living with all this misery has made me value life and all its opportunities. The opportunity I want more than any other is the chance to go to college.

Like Colby, many students described using challenging life experiences as motivating factors in their pursuit of health, happiness, and academic achievement.

Injury, Illness, and Death. Twenty-four percent of the essays described traumatic injuries or illnesses that students' family members experienced working in physically grueling conditions. Students revealed how these injuries and illnesses not only debilitated the parent or relative involved but also caused a traumatic downward cycle that pushed the entire family into poverty. Cynthia described a life-altering experience that took place when her father had a horrific accident at work and became permanently disabled:

> When my mom got the phone call informing her of my dad's accident, we couldn't believe it. We just thought my dad's friend was playing around. After the third time he called, we believed him. As we rushed to the hospital, all I could think about was that my fifteenth birthday party was ruined. I had so many questions on my mind: "Would my dad be okay? What would happen with my party? Would it be canceled?" All of my questions magically disappeared when I saw my dad suffering in the hospital bed, begging for help. My family did not know how to handle this life change.

Cynthia's father was the provider for her family, so his paralysis meant the family could no longer pay for their basic needs. Her mother eventually worked three jobs to pay the family's bills and support her husband's medical needs.

Students also wrote about the death of parents, siblings, and grandparents, and shared how losing loved ones changed their lives. Of suddenly losing his mother—and only caregiver—when he was 8 years old, Yobi wrote:

> My mom died of complications while giving birth to my little sister. My step-dad disliked me and my aunts and uncle did not want me. Three weeks after my mom passed away, my grandparents came from the United States to Guatemala. They started talking to me about how my mother had made them promise that they would care for me if anything were to happen to her. They came to take me to the United States. They broke the news to me slowly. My grandpa told me about the opportunities I would have and asked me, "Why don't you want to come with us? What's stopping you?" I responded, "My family and my brother and sister. I only have my brother and little sister left in this world." I didn't want to leave Guatemala.

Stories like Cynthia's and Yobi's represent authentic descriptions of students' experiences growing up in ethnically and linguistically diverse and low-income homes. Although these essay topics do not encompass all the experiences of urban youth from ethnically and linguistically communities, they are emblematic of the kinds of challenges these students face, as well as the strength, resiliency, and familial and aspirational capital these students bring to the classroom.

Extracurricular and Academic Support Programs

Thirty-six percent of the essays included descriptions of extracurricular activities or academic support programs that have taught students life lessons or fostered their academic success. The majority of the essays describing extracurricular programs shared stories of involvement in athletics.

Athletics. Seven students chose to focus their essays or a part of their essays on the ways sports have enriched their lives as students and as young men and women. For example, Rico wrote about his dream of attending college to give back to his family and community. He hoped to earn a scholarship for baseball as a way to repay those who have supported him throughout this life. He shared how playing baseball has influenced him to become a "better son, teammate, student, and friend" and taught him "to work as a teammate and to be a leader." Rico wrote about the way baseball has given him a "new way of seeing things." He described how baseball gave him a connection to school and to his teammates that he had never had before starting the sport. It also gave him clear goals to work toward as an athlete and a student.

> I have learned that through hard work and determination anything I set my mind to is possible. I improved my grades from a GPA of a 2.1 to a 3.05 and now I even have more credits than I need to graduate. My family and friends told me I would never be good enough to play in the North American Indigenous Games and that I am not smart enough to make it into a university, but I proved them all wrong. I played in the Indigenous Games and we won 4th place and I will attend a university. Baseball has proven to me that if I try my best and work hard, even with little support, I can do whatever I set my mind to and exceed my goals.

Like Rico, Gisele's involvement in extracurricular gymnastics helped shape her into the young woman she is today. She wrote, "Days to weeks, weeks to months, months to years went by. I continued my training. It was like my home. Coaches were like my parents and my teammates were my siblings." Gisele also described her struggle as a low-income

Mexican American participating in an expensive and predominately all-White sport.

> I never had the money to pay for fancy new leotards and I never had private lessons like the other girls on my team, but I found a way to excel at my sport through hard work and persistence. These are qualities I take with me wherever I go and help me succeed no matter what challenges I may face.

Gisele had an overwhelming desire to prove to everyone that she could be a gymnast and to "dazzle" her parents with her technique.

Academic support programs. Seventeen percent of the students focused some part of their essays on the positive influence of academic support programs such as:

a. AVID (refer to Chapter 3 for description)
b. Project ACES (a grant project sponsored by State Farm Insurance to provide awareness for prekindergarten through 12th grade and adults about motor vehicle and car seat and booster seat safety)
c. Model United Nations
d. Hispanic Mother–Daughter Program (academic support program for teenage girls and their mothers to increase the chances of Hispanic girls attending and graduating from college)
e. Rising Expectations in Academic and Community Service (REACH) (allows high school students to take college courses to help prepare for college).

Sarah, one of the students in Dan's class, wrote about how she used Model United Nations to overcome her fears about public speaking and feel confident in front of groups of people. She wrote,

> My first Model United Nations conference was held during the spring of 2008. I remember being nervous months before my conference and dreading the moment I would have to present my resolution to the rest of the assembly. Even after my preparation, the moment I had to stand up and walk to the podium to give Japan's view of the Palestinian refugees, I felt like I left myself. The walls started moving and I just saw faces yelling at me. I made it through my speech and sat down in a shocked stupor. I was not hurt; I had actually done it. At that moment I really felt I could conquer the world.

Sarah's essay goes on to describe how this experience with public speaking changed her perception of herself as a young woman: "I realized I can do things in my life even if they feel out of reach, intimidating, or scary. I can dig down deep and tap into my core strength and accomplish what I set out to do in life." Other students described programs such as the Hispanic Mother Daughter Program offered through the local university, the AVID program offered at the middle school and high school, and the REACH program offered through the local community college as powerful sponsors for their academic achievement. Students shared how these programs became "launching pads" for their academic growth or a "home base" to check in, set goals, and gain new information about moving on to college. Jared described his gratitude for the AVID program he was a part of in middle school: "AVID helped me improve my organizational skills and I learned simple things like it was much easier for me to find work in my backpack if my papers were not crumpled up anymore. This program made me determined to work even harder and to focus on my future goals."

The organizations and programs students were involved in had a significant impact on the experiences they had in school, the lessons they learned, and the relationships that fostered their development as individuals and as students.

Cultural and Ethnic Identity

Twenty-nine percent of the essays included connections with and participation in cultural and ethnic groups. Many of these stories were related to ethnic identity, immigration, and the cultural ties that bind families and communities who have immigrated to the United States. Students wrote about what it is like to belong to a marginalized ethnic group, as well as how these groups and the experiences that come from being a part of these groups have helped form their identities and sense of self. Within the broader theme of cultural and ethnic identities, we uncovered two subcategories: (1) ethnic identity and (2) immigration.

Negotiating Identity. Seventeen percent of the students demonstrated deftness with negotiating multiple cultural or ethnic identities in their writing. Rather than seeing themselves as members of a particular group—Mexican, American, Navajo, or Filipino—many of the students emphasized their membership in multiple cultural groups, as well as how they navigated different roles. Alejandro, for instance, wrote about what it was like to grow up as a light-skinned Latino in an all-White community:

> I developed my white skin throughout my years in school. Somehow I was still outcasted because my heart was brown. I don't

> have an accent, and my English is as perfect as your next white man. I speak my Spanish like a true Mexican but I'm not one of them either. I am Alejandro and my name is all that I am. . . . I am Alejandro, the Mexican American.

In his essay, Alejandro emphasized the struggles he faced feeling "too dark for some and too light for others." He maneuvered this struggle with his racial identity by showing his identity as an individual and as both a Mexican and American adolescent.

Dyani, like Alejandro, wrote about the importance of finding equanimity among her cultural identities. She wrote that her goal in life was attending college and "living the life as a Diné [Navajo]." Dyani said she has "learned so much from how our kinship clan system works, customs, stories/prayers, language, and livestock and nature" and, ideally, she wants to balance two cultures by living the "American way and Navajo way."

A few students wrote essays about proving to their families and to the world that they do not fit any "stereotype or statistic" and that they are "more than society gives them credit for." Gladys, for example, expressed pride in her ethnic heritage as a Latina woman but also sought to prove she would not fall into the stereotypical labels that stymie many young Latina women. She began her essay by recounting the dropout and pregnancy rates for Latina women. Then she shared a tale about the pressures her mother put on her to become a responsible, independent young woman and not "another pregnant Mexican teen." Gladys concluded her essay by emphasizing the lessons her mother taught her and her desire to "prove the world wrong" by showing that she is "more than any number or stereotype could ever be."

Other students used the essay as an opportunity to question the status quo by addressing the privileges and access many Americans have based on race and ethnicity. Carlos, for example, related his concerns that "skin color is the reason" immigrant youth of "all sizes and ages" are not able to "achieve their dreams and fall in bad steps" in life.

Through their essays, students demonstrated the role their ethnic identities have played in their lives, as well as the roadblocks they have had to face and overcome due to stereotypes and racism.

Immigration. Along with stories of ethnic identity, 12% of the students recounted tales of their own or their parents' immigration to the United States. The students shared the physical and emotional challenges of adjusting to a new culture and learning a new language. Jesus, who emigrated with his family from Guatemala, described how physical movement created emotional turmoil in his life. He also shared lessons learned from moving to a new country:

> People move for different reasons. Parents get a better job or they move to a better house. Yet when you're just a child, sometimes movement can affect you even more. As a child, moving means losing all of your friends, finding new ones, and going to a new school with new teachers. For me, moving has changed my life. I moved to the United States from Guatemala, which was the hardest, most beneficial move in my life. This move gave me a new perspective on life, language, and culture. It made me who I am today.

Carlos wrote about the general struggle caused by immigrating to a new country. He began his piece with a series of questions and comments regarding the challenges many Latinos face when immigrating to the United States. Carlos went on to address the fears many Latinos in the United States face with regard to deportation and the presence of police and immigration officials. He concluded his essay by saying that there will be roadblocks in life, like the struggles many Latinos face in immigrating to the United States, but to "never let these challenges interfere with your dreams." He also wrote that he has learned to "take the right path in life and not the wrong one after watching many immigrants fall to life's stresses and vices."

Jose focused his essay on how his perception of the United States shifted after he and his family moved to the United States from Mexico illegally when he was a young boy. He described in his essay how he went from believing anything was possible to understanding how challenging and terrifying life can be for undocumented immigrants. He also referred to the political turmoil surrounding issues of immigration in the state, which is discussed in further detail in Chapter 7.

> I always hear people tell me, "if you try hard lots of doors will open for you," but most of the people I know try and try and they don't see any doors nearby. Maybe this is because we are immigrants of all sizes, ages, and skin colors. We are not given opportunities to pursue our dreams. We live in a place with a sheriff who wants us deported. We live in fear of the police and we work for minimum wage and it feels like we are always running.

Through stories like Jose's, we learned more about the struggle, sacrifice, and upheaval students and their families have experienced as recent immigrants living in the United States. We also gained insight into how students' stories of immigration helped shape their perspective of the world, their vision of the future, and their understanding of equity and justice.

The Positive Role of Maternal Figures

Another theme was the positive influence of mothers, grandmothers, aunts, and older sisters on students' academic and personal success. Twenty-nine percent of the students wrote about how their mothers or other maternal figures served as primary sources of support and offered structure and encouragement despite limited education prior to emigrating from Mexico or other Latin America regions. For example, many students described how their mothers had sacrificed so they could go to school. Hector wrote about his mother's efforts when they were living in Mexico:

> For eight months we lived in a hollow house, eating beans and tortillas every day. My mother went to work at a jalapeno processing factory nearby. She left at six in the morning and returned at eight at night, with her delicate hands swollen, you could not distinguish her nails from her fingers.

Juan wrote about his parents' decision to leave Mexico City and move to the United States:

> It took an entire year for my mother, younger sister, and I to make it to the United States. Throughout that period of time, my mother cried blood, bled acid, and fought through constant battles so that my sister and I could stand where we are now.

During this year, Juan's mother was separated for large periods of time from her husband, extended family members, and children. She immigrated to the United States with Juan and left Juan's younger sister with family members in Mexico. Through much struggle, Juan's mother eventually returned to Mexico to bring Juan's sister to the United States and reunite the family.

Carmen also wrote about her relationship with her mother. She says that even though they have had their ups and downs, her mother is the person who has had the most positive influence on her life: "My mom is a really strong person and she never gives up. She always tells me to be determined and ambitious."

Angelica described the positive influence of her aunt who lives in Mexico. Even though she rarely spent time with her, Angelica looked up to her aunt because she had graduated from college in Mexico.

> My aunt is the youngest of seven children. Out of her six brothers and sisters, she was the only one that finished high school and went to college. She now has her degree and a full time job. She showed me that poverty shouldn't hold you back from doing what you love. She has very little, but she chose to study her passion. My aunt influenced me and gave me this motivation. I have made it through high school with her help and my next step is college.

Angelica explained that her aunt has served as an academic role model, but she has also shown her how to be a loving and caring person. She writes about her aunt taking care of her grandparents in Mexico and how her aunt values family over all other things in life. Angelica acknowledges at the end of her essay how she wants to follow in her aunt's footsteps: "I know I am barely starting my own life and I have a whole future ahead of me, but some of the steps I plan to take are the ones mi tia took before me."

Veneicia writes about the challenges she faced as a little girl raised by a single mother with limited resources:

> Some kids are lucky. Some are born into a stable, happy life. Those are the ones that take advantage of every opportunity that comes their way. But you look at the kids living with a single parent and realize they are often more thankful than the "lucky" child. I am a thankful child. Living with a single parent is a lifelong challenge. A lot of people may think it is no big deal, but in reality, it can be scary. I spent my childhood always having to worry if I would have enough money to pay the rent, or wonder who would watch me if my mom had to work.
>
> I grew up not knowing who my father was. He was never around and he probably never even knew I existed. My mom struggled with the rent and with expenses for me. Sometimes, we didn't have to worry about the rent because we were homeless. But then, somehow, my mom managed to pull it off and get us shelter. "I never asked to be in this situation so why is this happening to me?" That is the question I continually asked myself. Why did my life have to be so difficult and different from other people? I used to think God was punishing me for a mistake I made in a previous life. But, later in life, as I started growing and maturing, I realized that it was all just a test to see if I could face a challenge without giving up. And, I passed. I used to think I was a "thankful" child, but now I realize I am a lucky child. I have made it through life with only one parent. Yes, it was hard. But I did it and my mother is my inspiration.

Students were aware that there were limits to the kinds of cultural capital their parents could provide. However, rather than being discouraged by their mothers' struggles, students viewed their mothers' work ethic as a model of strength and resiliency.

VALUING STUDENTS' LANGUAGES

As we analyzed the essays, we gained a better sense of students' topic choices and we also noticed a trend that intersected or crossed the essay topics, which was the use of home or native languages, particularly Spanish and Native American languages. Although the state where this workshop took place is "English-only," meaning schools and teachers are required to privilege the English language over other languages in the classroom, 17% of the students made their home language an integral part of their essays. They drew on popular sayings from their home languages and cultures by incorporating the language into dialogue and conversation or by strategically intermingling two languages in a single phrase or sentence. In doing so, these students demonstrated linguistic flexibility and skillfulness with a variety of languages.

Dyani, for example, drew on her home language by opening her essay with "*Sa'ah Naaghai Bik'eh Hozhoo,*" a popular Navajo phrase that means living in harmony with nature and traveling a life path that is full of beauty. She said that she uses this phrase as a source of guidance as she navigates life. Dyani also emphasized that this phrase demonstrates how Navajo culture has shaped her cultural values. Later in the introductory paragraph, she drew on the Navajo phrase "*ta'a'whoo'jiteego.*" The English translation of this phrase roughly means, "It's up to you! Self-discipline, motivation, awareness, commitment that you yourself have to set in order to achieve your dreams and goals." Dyani used these phrases to set up the essay, which focused on the hardships she has faced, as well as how she has drawn strength from her Navajo culture and community to overcome these challenges. In doing so, Dyani used her home language and culture to establish a sense of identity in her essay.

Other students called upon their native language to share advice from and conversations with parents. Valeria included "*No hay mal que por bien no venga,*" or "no bad that good can't come from," in the introduction to her essay. This Spanish adage was a favorite of her mother's and had a dual purpose: to draw the reader into a narrative about a traumatic life event and to illustrate how her mother's words have taught Valeria to face life's troubles and persevere. Carlos used dialogue to capture the authenticity of childhood conversations with his father. Describing his father's work laying ground pipes for outdoor pools in "the hot Arizona sun," Carlos recounted his father telling him, *"Ahora no mijo; estoy muy cansado de el trabajo"* or "not today, my son; I'm too tired from work." Carlos went on to share how his life has improved over the years, thanks to his father's hard work and his commitment to family, which has taught Carlos the importance of family and learning from life's struggles.

One student, Alejandro, meshed codes by drawing on both English and Spanish, as well as the values he draws from both cultures. He wrote: "Whether I speak perfect English or not, 'cerveza' blood runs through my veins. But so does the burger I ate just yesterday on the streets of my town, where I live and will live for the rest of my life."

For the students we have discussed up to this point in connection with this theme, writing an essay for a college admissions panel about who they are as individuals meant weaving the languages they use in their daily lives into their writing. Through writing, students demonstrated the ways language practices are deeply connected to their individual identities and to the ways they hope to be perceived by a college admissions panel.

EMPOWERING STUDENTS TO TELL THEIR STORIES

As the examples in this chapter illustrate, the topics students shared in their college admission essays were deeply personal and self-revelatory and represented the kinds of victories and hardships students from ethnically and linguistically diverse communities face every day. As the research and teaching team gave students access to a real world, gate-opening writing task through the college admission essay workshop, we worked to build writing capital while honoring and celebrating the cultural capital students brought to this task. The research and teaching team made a conscious decision not to alter students' essay topics and, by doing so, made room for personal stories, lived experiences, and home languages. Teachers, curriculum specialists, and college admission officers are encouraged to find ways of rethinking and expanding their curriculum, teaching choices, and vision of what counts for real world, gate-opening writing, as the research and teaching team did in this workshop, to honor the rich resources that youth from ethnically and linguistically diverse communities have available outside of the classroom, and to value what they bring to educational institutions, as Hull and Schultz (2002) recommend.

In the workshop, students drew on school knowledge, as well as their own linguistic and cultural capital, to compose their admission essays.

This finding suggests the need for secondary teachers to find ways of incorporating students' home languages and personal tales into instruction on gate-opening writing genres, even if the voices and stories do not match the dominant narratives that are often deemed "official" in schools (Labov, 1972; Smitherman, 2006). As research has shown, it is important to acknowledge and honor the many different funds of knowledge young people draw from when they produce written texts (Moll, Amanti, Neff, & González, 1992; Street, 2005), even when these texts may have high stakes attached and are deeply rooted in the economic, educational, and racial privilege of dominant culture in the United States. By bringing students' "unofficial" or "unsanctioned" voices into the official classroom space, we can honor students' lived experiences and demonstrate their individual and cultural uniqueness (Gutiérrez, 2008).

We must also be willing to see students' facility and flexibility with languages (Paris, 2009; Rampton, 1998) and their counter-stories, which are personal stories or experiences with discrimination, resiliency, and pain (Solorzano & Yosso, 2002), as a gift rather than a hindrance that needs to be overcome or a barrier to success. This is especially important in states and communities where unofficial languages are not welcome or are banned from the classroom. Despite the arguably anti-immigrant sentiments of some of the political figures in the state where the workshop took place, students still chose to tell stories that focused on immigration, the resulting hardships and triumphs, and its role in forming their identities. These tales are indicative of the diverse experiences students bring to the classroom and the power of students' voices. To open the gates for all students to succeed after high school, students must be invited to share their stories through writing without fear of retribution or admonishment. The writing process is an ideal opportunity for students to explore their cultural and linguistic identities, as well as a chance to bring their voices to light and to make their perspectives known to broader audiences like college admissions panels.

As certain forms of cultural capital continue to be prized in academic institutions, we need to re-conceptualize whose voices and stories are included and valued within academic contexts. This is particularly true in the field of writing and literacy studies, where certain genres of writing continue to be considered more academically viable than others and instruction on how to write gate-opening genres, like the college admission essay, is too often offered only to secondary students who have been traditionally perceived of as "college-bound" or "college-ready" (Rodriguez & Cruz, 2009). We advocate for the inclusion of gate-opening writing genres in all secondary classrooms—regardless of level, track, or label—to provide access to the writing capital students need to move forward and succeed in academic and professional contexts. One step in this direction is to move beyond regimented, prescriptive, or traditional curriculum (see Kohn, 1999) by asking students to write about real issues, such as ethnic identity and immigration, for real audiences. Incorporating gate-opening writing tasks like the college admission essay, cover letters, interview questions and answers, and scholarship applications into the classroom may serve as another integral step toward honoring students' cultural capital and building their cultural writing capital. Furthermore, if colleges and universities hope to attract and retain students from ethnically, linguistically, and socially diverse backgrounds, then college admission officers, authors of guidebooks for the college admission essay, and guidance counselors should be not only aware of the kinds of stories that ethnically and linguistically diverse youth deem worthy of sharing in their admission essay, but also open to well-told narratives of any kind.

SUMMING UP

As educators, we can go beyond simply seeing students' diversity as something worth "honoring" and move toward action by cultivating curricular and instructional opportunities for students that allow them to make their voices known while also giving them access to life opportunities beyond classroom walls. This is the true essence of gate-opening writing: drawing on students' strengths and voices while helping to tear down the writing barriers that too often constrain our students. If we can begin to walk this fine line in our English classrooms, then the field of secondary language arts education can play a larger role in not only leveling the playing field but building a new field for all students. The following chapter extends Chapters 1 through 6 by exploring how to construct a classroom and school environment that fosters a culture of real world, gate-opening writing.

CHAPTER 7

Creating a Culture That Supports Real World, Gate-Opening Writing

Our task as educators is to assist people learning to assert their place in this world. We are their guides, coaches, and mentors as they learn to take place, find meanings, and accomplish work of personal and communal value. Our reward is to share in their pride and strength as their writing connects them with others.

—Charles Bazerman, 2010, p. 576

Drawing on and extending cultural capital and genre theories, as well as the work of literacy scholars like Charles Bazerman, this chapter examines the role that real world, gate-opening writing plays for students, classroom teachers, and researchers. The purpose is to illuminate the different positions and stakes these individuals have related to teaching and researching writing at the high school level. The chapter shares a reflection on the research process, including the relationships the research and teaching team developed during the study, the stakeholders we want to work more with, the external forces we were forced to negotiate, and the elements of the research process we have learned from and might shift or extend in future studies. The chapter also broadens the scope by exploring how these individuals may engage in dialogue and enact change in our schools by creating environments where all students learn real world, gate-opening writing tasks.

This book argues that college admission essays are one example of a genre of writing that can open gates for students by providing access to institutions of higher education, particularly for individuals who represent groups that have been held at the margins by the exercise of power. Efforts to demystify language and genre forms, which frequently function as reified forms of exclusion, are at the heart of teaching for social justice (Christensen, 2000, 2009; Kinloch, 2008; Morrell, 2007; Nieto, 2009). Providing students from underserved and underrepresented groups the tools to gain access into these exclusionary realms of discourse is a key part of teaching for social justice.

Often, discourses that channel power and maintain or perpetuate social inequalities are taken for granted by those who have access to these genres (Delpit, 1995; Delpit & Dowdy, 2002). Many high school teachers, for instance, assume that particular genre rules are already evident to their students or that these forms of discourse are simply unattainable, given the limited skills many students bring to high school due to challenging or disenfranchising learning experiences in elementary and junior high school. However, when teachers empower students to practice the skills needed to write real world genres, not only do students benefit from gaining access to the kinds of writing that have previously been withheld, but those in power learn from the rich experiences of those who have been marginalized. That is, genre rules can channel discourse in two directions and thus change individuals who have previously been on opposite sides of institutional boundaries.

Through this research, teaching, and writing, we do not want to diminish the importance of the multifaceted and valuable forms of real world writing that students already engage in through avenues such as texting, graffiti, tattooing, Twitter, or Facebook (Cintron, 1998; Fisher, 2007; Paris, 2010; Paris & Kirkland, 2011). In fact, professional and personal networking platforms like Twitter can cross over, and one of the goals of any critically conscious writing teacher is to understand and draw from the rich literacy practices and interests that students draw from their home and community lives.

In Maisha Fisher's (2007) study of ethnically and linguistically diverse secondary students engaged in spoken-word poetry workshops in urban classrooms, she takes the position that students must have avenues for building "literate identities" (p. 92). Her research illustrates how students must begin to "view themselves as literate, capable human beings who rightfully belong to a community of writers" (p. 83) and how teachers may support this identity formation by allowing students' home languages, cultures, and lived experiences into the classroom and into their writing. Our work with ethnically and linguistically diverse students writing college admission essays also points to the value of honoring students' voices and lived experiences. It also suggests that teachers of secondary writing may support and cultivate literate identities for ethnically and linguistically diverse students through the teaching of real world, gate-opening writing.

It is not enough to focus on and bridge personal or at-home literacies with the more "official" literacies of school. In Jeffrey Duncan-Andrade and Ernest Morrell's (2008) work on critical pedagogy, they call for teachers and researchers to "resist the urge to only focus on the emergence of critical consciousness without finding ways to link this consciousness to the development of academic skills" (p. 48). Whether students opt to participate in institutions of power, all students deserve to have access to the literacy skills needed to choose their life path. A critical aspect of teaching secondary literacy and cultivating literate identities for all students is providing access to the kinds of writing practices and experiences that are valued by institutions of power and that are deemed necessary to gain admission and access to higher education, the workplace, and the community. Many of these practices require sustained argumentation and explanation that cannot be communicated through brief genres such as text messages, graffiti, and tattoos.

This book extends the research studies and teaching projects of those such as Anne Beaufort (1999) and Kelly Gallagher (2011) by claiming that to teach real world and gate-opening writing is to ready students for the next stages of their lives. Giving students a range of writing experiences will not inherently prepare them for all the kinds of writing they will be asked to produce in their lifetimes, but it will offer them a better sense of the discourses, purposes, audiences, and genre elements required in these tasks. But being ready to write is also about imparting awareness to writing teachers and their students that these tasks function as gates that can be opened and accessed with careful attention, support, and sponsorship from mentors such as teachers, parents, and other members of school and local communities (Brandt, 2001). "Readiness" must come with an understanding of the genres themselves and the power structures and cultural capital related to writing real world and gate-opening genres.

LEARNING FROM ADOLESCENTS AS REAL WORLD WRITERS

The research and teaching team learned from students that writing, even when it is done for a real world audience beyond the self or the teacher, is personal. The research and teaching team were reminded of this as we helped teach the workshop, read essay drafts, met with students in writing conferences, and took part in the final celebration readings (a chance for every student to read his or her essay or an excerpt from the essay aloud to the class). At first, the research and teaching team figured many students would write about "typical" topics found in many admission essays, such as future career goals, travel to different locales, service opportunities, and extracurricular activities. However, the stories were more self-revelatory than anticipated, and rather than pretending that these topics were typical or forcing students to alter their topics to fit our perception of what counted as typical, the research and teaching team decided to embrace the deeply personal topics. Through the workshop, students were encouraged to write essays about their powerful lived experiences using genre expectations beyond topic choice as a guide. Through this research and teaching process, we learned that students have deeply personal stories to tell regardless of genre, and it is our task as researchers of writing to find ways to make these stories known to others in the literacy research and teaching community so the genre expectations of certain gate-opening writing tasks can expand to include diverse lived experiences, languages, and cultures.

The deeply personal nature of the students' stories is also an important piece of what it means to teach and study writing practices in secondary settings. If teachers choose to embed real world and gate-opening writing into the classroom, then we also must be prepared for the heartfelt topics, personal tales, and interests and aspirations of each student. If we want to address access and equity through writing, then we must, above all else, pay attention to individual writers to help them grow in their learning.

The need to focus on the individual writer became evident throughout the workshop, particularly during the teacher-student writing conferences, as students shared their needs and concerns relating to the college admission essay and application process. The research and teaching team held one-on-one conferences with every student toward the end of the workshop (Day 11) as a way to check in with individual writers regarding progress, to answer students' questions, and to provide feedback and suggestions for revision. During these conferences, many students asked for and wanted reassurance above all else. For example, when Jessica sat across from Jackie and asked what she wanted or hoped to receive from the conference, Jackie replied:

> I just want to know that this story is okay to share. I just don't know if it makes any sense or if anyone will really care what I have to say or what happened in my life.

She explained that the biggest challenge she faced during the workshop was "just believing in myself." For Jackie, having a chance to meet with teachers and professors about her writing made her feel like her writing mattered and that others believed in her. After her conference with Jessica, Jackie asked if she could have another conference with a different member of the teaching team. She said she wanted as much help as she could get. For Jackie, the conferences gave her an opportunity to seek support and reinforcement for her work, something she was aware she needed as a writer.

The research and teaching team also found that a number of students who had been shy or quiet during the workshop were forthcoming and sociable in the writing conferences. For example, Jerman never spoke aloud to address the class or the teaching team during the workshop sessions. As he took part in the workshop, he asked a few times if it was okay to listen to music with his headphones while he wrote. The research and teaching team chose to allow this as a practice as long as he was writing and the music did not disrupt others. This turned out to be a useful way to support his writing needs. In his writing conference, he asked Arturo, one of the doctoral students on the teaching team, if he could share his guitar. Jerman had brought his guitar to class every day but had never talked about it or shared his love for music until the conference day. During his conference, Jerman showed off his guitar and talked to Arturo about the way music had served as a source of inspiration and support in his young life. Arturo suggested that Jerman incorporate this in some way into this college admission essay. The conference gave Jerman an opportunity to comfortably share an interest and passion that turned out to be an important contribution to his writing. It also gave Arturo an opportunity to learn more about Jerman as a young musician.

Above all else, the conversations the research and teaching team had with students and the writing students shared and produced in the workshop were reminders that there is a lot at stake when we teach real world and gate-opening writing. Students were not only invested in writing the college admission essays as a part of a writing workshop, but they perceived this writing as a means of improving their lives and of proving something to themselves and to their families. Many students shared the ways that writing for a college audience "felt like a big responsibility." For example, in a reflection written after the workshop, Alfredo shared that writing the college admission essay made him feel hopeful about his future. He wrote:

> To me, a college education means freedom and it means having the freedom to be anything and anyone in life. A college education would make me the first in my family of seven to graduate from high school and pursue a higher degree. I want to set an example for my little brothers and sisters.

Student Jessica also shared in her final reflection how writing the essay meant more than just completing an assignment and earning a grade for class:

> Most of my life, I have always been looked down on by my father's side of the family. Whether it has been because of my personal interests or the fact that I was a "mistake" or, in other words, born out of wed lock. Since the start of my academic career, my single mother and I have always strived to achieve the best grades and the highest class ranks in my education. A college education not only would be an opportunity to live a better life with a better income, but for me, personally, it's a way of proving myself to my family. No matter what my interests are, no matter the legal status of my parents, if I set my mind on something I will achieve it.

Throughout the workshop, students reminded the research and teaching team that learning this real world, gate-opening writing task was about sharing personal and sometimes difficult stories, progressing as individual writers, persisting to college despite life's challenges, and making efforts to better their own and their family's lives.

As is the case in all schools, students came to this writing task with a range of skills and experiences and this range was magnified by the linguistic diversity in the classroom. As Jessica and Meredith analyzed student writing once the workshop was complete, they took into consideration some of the obstacles and challenges that secondary English teachers face in their daily work with students in diverse, crowded, and busy classrooms.

Although many students carefully blended their home languages into their essays (described in Chapter 6), we also noticed how some students struggled with their writing fluency. First, a couple of students' final essays did not extend beyond a single paragraph or only listed a number of personal or academic accomplishments, which meant that the essays were not as thorough or clear as we had hoped for their final draft. Further, because the college application prompt is broad and asks students to write about any number of issues related to the self and life goals, a few students struggled to write to a specific prompt. As a result, their final essays became an amalgamation of many prompts rather than a focused, clear essay addressing a single topic or question. Alex, for instance, wrote about his:

a. Native American heritage and the diversity he could add to the university
b. experience with a school academic program that has served as a source of guidance
c. family history of substance abuse, which he vowed to stay away from.

Other students embedded descriptions of family members who have influenced their character, extracurricular activities, traumatic life events, and economic hardships into an essay. This meant that while some of the essays included compelling content, there were a few essays that were ultimately not cohesive because they attempted to tackle too many topics without enough depth.

Writing fluency was another issue for some of the linguistically diverse students in the workshop. A few students had recently immigrated to the United States from Mexico and were in the process of learning to speak and write in English, particularly in academic contexts. Other students, who were not immigrants, simply struggled to compose smooth, fluent sentences. Many of these students were not accustomed to standard or dominant forms of English. Because learning any language takes time and the research and teaching team wanted students to see this task as one step, among many, toward learning English, fluency was not our primary concern. However, the research and teaching team knew that fluency might be a concern for a college admission officer looking for correctness in the essay.

LEARNING FROM TEACHERS WORKING IN TUMULTUOUS TIMES

As described in Chapter 3, the classroom teachers were unique in their approach to teaching and in their manner and style with students. Sarah and Dan embraced this project from a place of inquiry and enthusiasm. At the time this study took place, however, they were encountering overwhelming pressure from external forces such as internal departmental and school demands, district mandates and statewide literacy testing, and the complicated and systemic fallout from local and statewide immigration politics. The collaboration on this study took place at a time when real world political issues and policies formed a highly charged, contentious, and complex backdrop for this work.

ARIZONA POLITICS AS A BACKDROP

Arizona has recently been featured in national headlines as the epicenter of national immigration politics as a result of current governor Jan Brewer's controversial "Support Our Law Enforcement and Safe Neighborhoods Act," Arizona State Senate Bill 1070 (2010). As noted in Chapter 3, the law, which requires police to question a person's citizenship if they have reason to doubt an individual is in the country legally, sparked a national debate about the civil rights of individuals. Arizona communities from Flagstaff to Tucson have been in a state of turmoil, with ethnically and linguistically diverse families of all citizenship statuses questioning their ability to continue living in the state. Some classroom teachers beyond those who participated in this study have even reported that their students fear for their safety, realizing that their parents could be deported at any time. And these teachers have been faced with a daunting task: convincing their ethnically and linguistically diverse students that they are safe and entitled to an education in this state. At the time of the study, Libertad High School was experiencing the highest numbers of absences it had ever experienced, and the teachers and administrators explained that many students were not planning to return. (Many undocumented families did not feel safe sending their sons and daughters to school and were choosing to find work in other states.)

Arizona governor Jan Brewer had also recently signed Arizona State House Bill 2281 (2010) into law. As noted in Chapter 3, this law prohibits K–12 public schools from teaching courses that "are designed primarily for pupils of a particular ethnic group"—in other words, any ethnic studies or non-European-centered accounts of U.S. or Arizona history. According to the law, ethnic studies courses "promote the overthrow of the United States government or promote resentment toward a race or class of people." "Ethnic solidarity" is named as a threat to the state. Like Arizona State Senate Bill 1070 (2010), this legislation arguably demonizes non-White immigrants.

The metropolitan area where this study took place has also been the target of "immigration sweeps" by federal and especially county enforcement officers. The leader of these sweeps is Maricopa County's present sheriff, Joe Arpaio, who calls himself "America's Toughest Sheriff" and is known for his hard-nosed stance against undocumented immigrants. This has resulted in regular police surveillance of predominately Hispanic communities. Teachers Jessica has worked with beyond those who participated in the study have stated that they find that many of their students are transient and apt to disappear.

Arizona voters passed a ballot initiative in 2000 that required all English language learners to be educated through structured English immersion (SEI) programs, which means students who are not fluent in English are placed in classes separate from fluent English speakers with the idea that this structure will help students learn English quickly. These programs are provided and authored by the Arizona Department of Education and can only be modified with explicit written consent.

Given such a complex and challenging backdrop for their teaching, Sarah and Dan felt strained. For example, one of the first conversations Jessica had with them when she was scheduling the workshop was about the new state immigration laws and their influence on students and teaching. Sarah and Dan told Jessica that they had a number of undocumented students in their classes (they could not provide a number because this information is confidential) and they worried that these students would feel disenfranchised by the curriculum of this workshop. Although it is illegal for teachers or any school officials to ask students about their immigration status, both teachers explained that this was an "elephant in the room." Some students were willing to talk about or write about it, but they, as teachers, did not always know how to respond. Sarah and Dan both welcomed the workshop on the college admission essay for all of their students and they hoped that this project would give undocumented students, as well as all the other students, access to information and skills they would need to move forward with their schooling. No one on the research and teaching team could anticipate the reactions and outcomes of the workshop on the college admission essay, but Sarah and Dan were well aware from the onset of this project that teaching the workshop on this real world and gate-opening genre, although seemingly innocuous, was in fact highly political and charged.

In 2006, Arizona citizens passed State of Arizona Proposition 300, which prohibits undocumented students from qualifying for in-state tuition and state financial aid. For the undocumented students in the class, this legislation extinguished their plans and hopes for higher education. Although every student who participated in the workshop reported that they wanted to go to college, as described in Chapter 1, financial pressures were both personal and political for this group of students. With this in mind, the research and teaching team made a conscious effort to provide all students with information regarding scholarships and financial aid packages, as well as strategies to access financial support that was not state-funded. Sara, the undergraduate college student who worked on the research team, researched grants, fellowships, and awards the high school students could apply for to support their pursuit of higher education. She also made a brochure that the research and teaching team handed out to both classes with information from the state colleges and universities regarding scholarships for ethnically and linguistically diverse students. Although these efforts could not erase the challenges, fears, and anxieties revolving around this task for the teachers and students, they served as starting points to navigate this tumultuous time in Arizona and U.S. history and to open the gates of access to students.

Given this social and political environment, teaching and learning college admission essay writing was a political act and, to some extent, a defiant one. The workshop functioned as a form of writing sponsorship for students. The curriculum, research and teaching team, and materials all worked to communicate that there were adults and institutions that were not overtly discriminatory and were striving to be supportive of the students' aspirations. This kind of support for students' experiences and dreams can function as a way to bolster their resilience in the face of long odds against them. By supporting ethnically and linguistically diverse students' aspirations through writing, literacy teachers serve as the kind of sponsors who appear to be essential for promoting resilience in adolescents (Brandt, 2001; Werner & Smith, 1992, 2001). The personal nature of the material students chose to reveal in their essays—stories that they had not previously disclosed to their teachers—was evidence that they perceived the classroom and the teachers as safe and supportive.

In Sonia Nieto's (2009) words, teaching for social justice means

> providing all students with the resources necessary to learn to their full potential. This includes *material resources* such as books, curricula, financial support, and so on. Equally vital are *emotional resources* such as a belief in students' ability and worth, care for them as individuals and learners, high expectations and rigorous demands on them, and the necessary social and cultural capital to negotiate the world. (p. 46)

The curriculum for this workshop functioned in a way that allowed students to feel that school was a place that not only honored their lived experiences but also helped demystify a genre of writing that may help open doors to their future lives and aspirations. Sarah and Dan's support for and dedication to this workshop and, on a broader sense, their unwavering commitment to providing students' access to real world, gate-opening writing forms—despite the contentious political climate in the state and mounting testing and accountability pressures—are concrete reminders of what it means to teach for and work toward social justice in education.

LEARNING FROM THE RESEARCH PROCESS

Although much of this book combines a teaching and research story, there were lessons learned specifically connected to the work of researching writing. As we began to negotiate the research process, the research team experienced the balancing act that must occur when researching writing in the secondary classroom. Researchers must negotiate different roles; communicate and collaborate with different stakeholders; collect, protect, and organize written material; and remain true to an overarching or guiding research question and stance.

Compiling and Organizing Writing

Through the research process, the research team learned lessons about the process of collecting and analyzing student writing within a classroom setting. First, we found a number of strategies and materials useful for collecting and making sense of student writing:

a. space to make piles and spread out data
b. sticky notes to numerically tally the codes, to flag interesting topics that did not fit in with others, and to organize the writing in stacks
c. Google Docs for analyzing, listing, and coding topics
d. bins and folders to separate classes and types of writing weekly email check-ins with the research and teaching teams to talk about the research process, set up next steps for data collection, and problem solve and strategize.

Even though these methods for collecting and analyzing data were useful, the research team realized ways to improve on some elements in the future. One of the things we would do differently is to have a more user-friendly system for collecting, filing, and storing written work. The process of collecting student writing, stripping all identifiers, coding writing with student-specific numbers after stripping their names, copying writing, and filing writing from two classes proved to be more complicated than we had anticipated.

As a former high school English teacher, Jessica had had plenty of experience collecting and keeping track of large numbers of student papers and she had anticipated the need for a system of collecting student work. She initially considered purchasing flash drives for each student, which would allow them to save written work after every workshop session. However, after meeting with Sarah and Dan prior to the study, she learned students would not have daily access to computers and could not safely store material on school computers without it getting erased by the main server every night. Jessica instead purchased portfolio folders for each student to file written work and to organize all workshop handouts, free-writes, and information. These folders were passed out at the beginning of every class and collected at the end of every class. (Students never took work home from the workshop because we were concerned we could lose track of their written work or lose key drafts or reflections. Jessica was also concerned about maintaining confidentiality and protecting the data.) Between classes, all portfolios remained in a locked filing cabinet in Jessica's research office. Arturo was responsible for collecting and transporting all written documents between Libertad and the university. Arturo and Jessica made hard copies of student work for Sarah and Dan to use for grading or keeping track of participation and attendance.

Because the research team gathered so many different kinds of student writing from two separate classes, including multiple drafts of the college admission essay, in-class writing related to the workshop, and questionnaires, it was a difficult juggling act to keep all the files in order and move through the analysis of student writing while keeping the data secure and safe in Jessica's office. We learned that it is important not only to have an organizational system in place but to practice using this system to ensure it works for the research and teaching teams. In the future, as a study unfolds, we plan to scan and save the files as PDFs to prevent having endless stacks of student writing at the end of the study. Jessica had not anticipated how difficult it would be to keep so many hard copies of student writing in order. Each time an essay was removed from a folder, the research team had to take time to find the proper code and place it back in the correct file in the right order. This would have been much easier to negotiate using a computer filing system. We also plan to use cloud or online-based tools such as Google Docs, Dropbox, or Box, which would allow the research team to securely store and access files without having to go to a separate location. It also affords the team the chance to archive the material for future use and draw on it from any computer with an Internet connection as it is needed for teaching, service, or publication projects. These were a few of the lessons learned about the unique nature of collecting, analyzing, and protecting writing samples for this study.

Gaining Access to Conduct Research

Jessica received permission from the school administrators, school district, and university Internal Review Board prior to the study. She also collected the proper releases from students, parents, and teachers prior to the workshop. However, she was continually reminded during her time at Libertad that access to a research site is not simply gaining permission to conduct the research. Access must be revisited daily and earned over time by developing trusting relationships with the network of students, parents, and school staff—including administrators, secretaries, janitors, and parking staff—we interacted with every day.

Having our research and teaching team enter Libertad to work with teachers and students required work on the part of the administrators, who had to follow a set of steps and protocols required of any school leader when opening the school to outsiders. Although Jessica had received permission from the principal to conduct the study at the university, school district, school, and classroom levels, she still had to work alongside the research and teaching team to communicate the purpose for the project each time any of us entered the school building. For example, Jessica, Arturo, and Cynthia arrived at Libertad one morning, checked in at the front office with the secretary, and began the long walk to the back of the school where one of the classrooms was located. Jessica, Arturo, and Cynthia had arrived during a passing period, and the corridor was bustling with students. The security guard and principal were patrolling the hallways and did not recognize us in the midst of the noise and commotion. The security guard stopped Jessica and asked to see her guest pass, at which point she and Arturo and Cynthia showed their passes and explained the purpose of the visit to campus. Although the principal felt terrible about the security guard not recognizing the research team, she also said, "I always have to ask to double-check that people are who they say they are and that my school is safe." This was a reminder, among many the research team experienced during our time at Libertad, that no matter what efforts we made to take on an emic perspective, we were outsiders entering a pre-established learning community. It was part of our work as researchers to follow the protocol and rules of the school while also remaining focused on the study's research questions and the intent of the study. Our experiences with the school administrators represent the ways in which researchers must work with the many layers of individuals involved in the teaching of writing at the secondary level.

CONSIDERING NEXT STEPS

This book details one example of a real world, gate-opening writing workshop and highlights the student voices and writing that emerged during that workshop. However, there are many more stories to tell related to the teaching and learning of real world, gate-opening writing genres in the secondary classroom and there are many questions left to pursue (see lingering questions in Chapter 4). It would be useful, for instance, to engage in the following research:

a. a case study of a particular teacher who implements real world, gate-opening writing in the classroom, why that teacher wants to embed these writing tasks into the curriculum, and what that teaching process looks like

b. a case study of a student or group of students as they navigate the process of learning how to write another real world, gate-opening writing genre
c. an interview study that explores the words and perspectives of those involved in creating a school culture that supports real world, gate-opening writing
d. a quantitative study that analyzes surveys completed by teachers or students who take part in real world, gate-opening writing workshops
e. a longitudinal study of an English department working to implement more real world and gate-opening into their curriculum and the challenges and successes connected to this work.

To that end, more transformative curricular work is needed like the study described in Chapters 1 through 6, where researchers, teachers, and students come together to bring real world, gate-opening writing into the space of the secondary classroom.

What does it mean to create a culture that supports real world, gate-opening writing in secondary schools? It is every student's right to gain access to, learn about, and practice the kinds of writing they will likely encounter in their future lives as students, employees, and citizens. Through the research team's time at Libertad High School collaborating with teachers, administrators, and students to examine a real world, gate-opening writing workshop, we also came to understand how creating a culture to support this kind of work is not a solitary act. Through the teaching of real world and gate-opening writing, secondary language arts teachers are in positions of remarkable power and possibility. They may work to shape the lives of their students and help them imagine, access, and work toward their future selves and life aspirations.

To extend real world writing activities beyond individual classrooms, it is important to foster administrative, faculty, and staff buy-in. To do this, teachers must encourage administrators; other faculty, particularly those who teach English language arts; and staff members to understand the purposes behind teaching these writing tasks and the important role these tasks play in students' present and future lives. This means sitting down with colleagues to tell them about the work going on in the classroom and communicating which tasks students are learning and why. Open lines of communication are key. This will help ensure that students' experiences with real world, gate-opening writing become embedded into the school's culture rather than viewed as an add-on or a "special" unit in one teacher's classroom.

It is also imperative that teachers relate to their administrators and fellow faculty how important it is to extend writing beyond standardized testing prompts. If teachers want students to truly be prepared for life after high school, then they must emphasize an expanded view of what counts as writing. Genres such as narratives, literary analyses, and timed writing responses all have a time and place in the educational process, but they are not the only writing genres. Real world genres should count, and educators would do well to bring more of those into the classroom.

SUMMING UP

This book represents both a culmination and a starting point for observers, teachers, and researchers of secondary writing. One of the first questions people ask Jessica in response to this work from Libertad is if she followed up with students after the workshop to see how many applied to and attended college. Although this is a logical question, it is also challenging to respond to. On the one hand, it makes sense to wonder if the students used the essay in the real world—that is, to apply to and gain acceptance to college. This, in the end, is the real-life application, purpose, and audience for this work. In the months following the workshop, Sarah and Daniel did share with Jessica and Arturo that all of their students applied to college and many used the essays for their applications or scholarships. However, Jessica chose not to trace the number of students who went to college or persisted in their schooling. This was never the purpose of this work; the goal was to expose students to a new form of writing that might help them as they work toward college. Furthermore, Jessica wanted students to view this workshop as much more than a series of quick get-into-college activities. She wanted to demonstrate that writing is a powerful literacy tool that can be used to support access and equity in our schools, particularly for students who have been marginalized in their educational endeavors. The process of getting into college is not easy. This research and teaching journey highlights that learning and practicing the college admission essay genre is one of the many important steps students must take to persist toward college and to open the gates of opportunity.

Educators at all levels must believe in the role writing can play in transforming the lives of students. The students at Libertad illustrate that learning to write a particular genre for a specific audience not only can influence their ability to write in that genre but also foster their writing confidence and pride. If educators believe students and their cultures are worth valuing, then they must find ways to honor students' lives in the classroom and the writing curriculum. Educators must do much more than simply say that they "honor" students and their cultural practices. They must view students' lives as worthy of writing about, and they must encourage students to share their stories, ideas, inquiries, and arguments with the world. Above all, educators must offer students access to new forms of writing, ones that can rotate the axis of equity. Throughout this book, we have tried to show the power of real world, gate-opening genres as a way of expanding students' writing repertoires and giving them the opportunity to experience the writing that takes place in the real world. As we have shown, doing so can have a profound impact on students' lives.

APPENDIX A

College Admission Essay Workshop Schedule

WEEK 1

Day 1 (Monday)

Introduce the workshop, hand out first questionnaire on General Experiences Writing the College Admission Essay and Writing Self-Efficacy Survey Pre-Workshop, and have students complete.

Day 2 (Wednesday)

Students write initial draft of the college admission essay using the Common Application prompts.

WEEK 2

Day 3 (Monday)

Begin working draft of the essay and pre-writing. Introduce skill lesson: selecting a strong writing topic.

Day 4 (Wednesday)

Expand upon initial draft and introduce skill lesson: getting to know your audience.

WEEK 3

Day 5 (Monday)

Introduce skill lesson: writing an effective introduction.

Day 6 (Wednesday)

Introduce skill lesson: using description.

WEEK 4

Day 7 (Monday)

Work on introductions and body of essay using description.

Day 8 (Wednesday)

Introduce skill lesson: sharing your "So What?" text and conclusions.

WEEK 5

Day 9 (Monday)

Writing conferences and revision.

Provide time for typing in the computer lab.

Day 10 (Wednesday)

Introduce skill lesson: revision and peer review.

WEEK 6

Day 11 (Monday)

Introduce skill lesson: writing effective conclusions.

Begin final draft of the essay.

Writing conferences and revision, time for typing in the computer lab.

Day 12 (Wednesday)

Students participate in final read-aloud.

Students work on final draft of the college admission.

Day 13 (Friday)

Students fill out Questionnaire: Writing Self-Efficacy Post-Workshop and Post-Workshop Reflection: final Reflection about learning to write the college admission essay.

Introduce undergraduate panel from the local university.

Hand out workshop completion certificate.

APPENDIX B

Post-Workshop Reflection

1. What are three things you learned from this workshop about writing college admission essays?
2. What are three things you learned from this workshop about applying to college?
3. How comfortable do you feel applying to college and writing admissions essays now that you have completed this workshop? Please explain.
4. What obstacles do you feel may stand in the way of you going to college? Please explain.
5. Is there anything you still want to know or need help with in applying for college or writing an admission essay?
6. Additional comments:

References

ACT. (2005). Crisis at the core: Preparing all students for college and work [Electronic Version]. Retrieved from http://www.act.org/path/policy/alert/crisis.html

Agee, J. M. (1995). Making connections with poetry: Multicultural voices in process. *Teaching English in the Two-Year College, 22*(1), 54–60.

American Diploma Project. (2004). *Ready or not: Creating a high school diploma that counts*. Washington, DC: Achieve.

Applebee, A. N., & Langer, J. A. (2009). What's happening in the teaching of writing? *English Journal, 98*(5), 18–28.

Arizona Department of Education. (2008). *Arizona department of education school report cards*. Retrieved from http://www10.ade.az.gov/ReportCard/

Arizona House Bill, 2281, *H.R.*, art. 1 chap. 1 § 15 (2010) (enacted). Retrieved March 30, 2012, from http://www.azleg.gov/legtext/49leg/2r/bills/hb2281s.pdf

Arizona Proposition 300, art. 2 chap. 14 § 4.15 (2006).

Atwell, N. (1987). *In the middle: Writing, Reading, and learning with adolescents*. Portsmouth, NH: Boynton/Cook.

Ball, A. F. (2000). Empowering pedagogies that enhance the learning of multicultural students. *Teachers College Record,* 102, 1006–1034.

Ball, A. F. (2006). Teaching writing in culturally diverse classrooms. In C. A. MacArthur, S. Graham, & J. Fitzgerald (Eds.), *The handbook of writing research* (pp. 293–310). New York: Guilford Press.

Bandura, A. (1986). *Social foundations of thought and action: A social cognitive theory*. Englewood Cliffs, NJ: Prentice Hall.

Bauld, H. (2005). *On writing the college application essay: Secrets of a former Ivy League admissions officer*. New York: Collins.

Bazerman, C. (1997). The life of genre, the life in the classroom. In H. Ostrom (Ed.), *Genres and writing: Issues, arguments, alternatives* (pp. 19–26). Portsmouth, NH: Heinemann.

Bazerman, C. (2004). Speech acts, genres, and activity systems: How texts organize activity and people. In C. Bazerman & P. Prior (Eds.), *What writing does and how it does it: An introduction to analyzing texts and textual practices* (pp. 309–339). Mahwah, NJ: Lawrence Erlbaum.

Bazerman, C. (2010). 2009 CCCC chair's address: The wonder of writing. *College Composition and Communication, 61*(3), 571–580.

Bazerman, C., & Prior, P. (2005). Participating in emergent socio-literate worlds: Genre, disciplinarity, interdisciplinarity. In R. Beach, J. Green, M. Kamil, & T. Shanahan (Eds.), *Multidisciplinary perspectives on literacy research* (2nd ed., pp. 133–178). Cresskill, NJ: Hampton Press.

Beaufort, A. (1999). *Writing in the real world: Making the transition from school to work*. New York: Teachers College Press.

Bourdieu, P. (1984). *Distinction: A social critique of the judgement of taste* (R. Nice, Trans.). Cambridge, MA: Harvard University Press. (Original work published 1979)

Bourdieu, P., & Passeron, J. C. (1977). Cultural reproduction and social reproduction. In J. Karabel & A. H. Halsey (Eds.), *Power and ideology in education* (pp. 487–511). New York: Oxford University Press.

Brandt, D. (2001). *Literacy in American lives*. Cambridge, United Kingdom: Cambridge University Press.

Carbonaro, W., & Gamoran, A. (2002). The production of achievement inequality in high school English. *American Educational Research Journal, 34*(4), 801–827.

Carvalho, J. B. (2002). Developing audience awareness in writing. *Journal of Research in Reading, 23*(3), 271–282.

Charney, D. H., & Carlson, R. A. (1995). Learning to write in a genre: What student writers take from model texts. *Research in the Teaching of English, 29*(1), 88–125.

Cheng, A. (2008). Analyzing genre exemplars in preparation for writing: The case of an L2 graduate student in the ESP genre-based instructional framework of academic literacy. *Applied Linguistics, 29*(1), 50–71.

Christensen, L. (2000). *Reading, writing, and rising up: Teaching about social justice and the power of the written word*. Milwaukee, WI: Rethinking Schools.

Christensen, L. (2009). *Teaching for joy and justice: Re-imagining the language arts classroom*. Milwaukee, WI: Rethinking Schools.

Cintron, R. (1998). *Angels' town: Chero ways, gang life, and rhetorics of the everyday*. Boston: Beacon Press.

College Board. (n.d.). *Sample college essay questions*. Retrieved December 7, 2011, from http://www.collegeboard.com/student/apply/essay-skills/108.html

The Common Application. (n.d.a). *2010–11 first-year application*. Retrieved December 7, 2011, from https://www.commonapp.org/CommonApp/Docs/DownloadForms/CommonApp2011.pdf

The Common Application. (n.d.b). *History*. Retrieved December 8, 2011, from https://www.commonapp.org/CommonApp/History.aspx

Compton-Lilly, C. (2009). The development of habits over time (WCER Working Paper No. 2009-7). Madison: University of Wisconsin–Madison, Wisconsin Center for Education Research. Retrieved October 22, 2010, from http://www.wcer.wisc.edu/publications/workingPapers/papers.php

Cope, B., & Kalantizis, M. (1993). *The power of literacy: A genre approach to teaching writing*. Pittsburgh, PA: University of Pittsburgh Press.

Cope, B., & Kalantizis, M. (Eds.). (2000). *Multiliteracies: Literacy learning and the design of social futures*. London: Routledge.

Creswell, J. W. (1998). *Qualitative inquiry and research design: Choosing among five traditions*. London: Sage.

Davis, A., Clarke, M. A., & Rhodes, L. K. (1994). Extended text and the writing proficiency of students in urban elementary schools. *Journal of Educational Psychology, 86*(4), 556–566.

Dean, D. (2008). *Genre theory: Teaching, writing, and being*. Urbana, IL: National Council of Teachers of English.

Delpit, L. (1995). *Other people's children: Cultural conflict in the classroom*. New York: The New Press.

Delpit, L., & Dowdy, J. K. (2002). *The skin that we speak: Thoughts on language and culture in the classroom*. New York: The New Press.

DiMaggio, P. (1982). Cultural capital and school success: The impact of status culture participation on the grades of U.S. high school students. *American Sociological Review, 47*(2), 189–201.

Donovan, C. A., & Smolkin, L. B. (2006). Children's understanding of genre and writing. In C. A. MacArthur, S. Graham, & J. Fitzgerald (Eds.), *The handbook of writing research* (pp. 131–143). New York: Guilford Press.

Duke, N. K. (2000). 3.6 minutes per day: The scarcity of informational texts in first grade. *Reading Research Quarterly, 35*(2), 202–224.

Duncan-Andrade, J. M. R., & Morrell, E. (2008). *The art of critical pedagogy: Possibilities for moving from theory to practice in urban schools*. New York: Peter Lang.

Dyson, A. H., & Genishi, C. (2005). *On the case: Approaches to language and literacy research*. New York: Teachers College Press.

Early, J. S. (2010). "Mi'ja, you should be a writer": Latino parental support of their first-generation children. *Bilingual Research Journal, 33*(3), 277–291.

Early, J. S., & Shagoury, R. (2010). Learning from the lived experiences of new language arts teachers working in diverse, urban schools. *Teaching and Teacher Education, 26*(4), 1049–1058.

Edelsky, C. (1986). *Writing in a bilingual program: Habla una vez*. Norwood, NJ: Ablex.

Englert, C. S., Stewart, S. R., & Hiebert, E. H. (1988). Young writers' use of text structure in expository text generation. *Journal of Educational Psychology, 80*(2), 143–151.

Faltis, C., & Wolfe, P. (Eds.). (1999). *So much to say: Adolescents, bilingualism, and ESL in the secondary school*. New York: Teachers College Press.

Fisher, M. T. (2007). *Writing in rhythm: Spoken word poetry in urban classrooms*. New York: Teachers College Press.

Fiske, E. B., & Hammond, B. G. (2009). *Fiske real college essays that work, second edition*. Naperville, IL: Sourcebooks.

Fitzgerald, J., & Teasley, A. B. (1986). Enhancing children's writing through instruction in narrative structure. *Journal of Educational Psychology, 78*(6), 424–432.

Freedman, A. (1993). Show and tell? The role of explicit teaching in the learning of new genres. *Research in the Teaching of English, 27*(3), 22–51.

Gallagher, K. (2011). *Write like this: Teaching real world writing through modeling and mentor texts*. Portland, ME: Stenhouse.

Gandara, P., & Rumberger, R. (2009). Immigration, language, and education: How does language policy structure opportunity? *Teachers College Record, 111*(3), 750–782.

García, S. B., & Guerra, P. L. (2004). Deconstructing deficit thinking: Working with educators to create more equitable learning environments. *Education and Urban Society, 36*(2), 150–168.

Geertz, C. (1973). *The interpretation of cultures*. New York: Basic Books.

Gelb, A. (2008). *Conquering the college admissions essay in 10 steps: Crafting a winning personal statement*. New York: Ten Speed Press.

Gelband, S., Kubale, C., & Schorr, E. (1986). *Your college application*. New York: College Board.

Graham, S., & Harris, K. (2005). *Writing better: Effective strategies for teaching students with learning difficulties*. Baltimore: Paul H. Brookes.

Graham, S., & Perin, D. (2007). A meta-analysis of writing instruction for adolescent students. *Journal of Educational Psychology, 99*(3), 445–476.

Guerra, J. C. (1998). *Close to home: Oral and literate practices in a transnational Mexicano community*. New York: Teachers College Press.

Gutiérrez, K. (2008). Developing a sociocritical literacy in the third space. *Reading Research Quarterly, 43*(2), 148–164.

Hackett, G. (1995). Self-efficacy in career choice and development. In A. Bandura (Ed.), *Self-efficacy in changing societies* (pp. 232–258). New York: Cambridge University Press.

Hansen, J. (1998). *When learners evaluate*. Portsmouth, NH: Heinemann.

The Harvard Crimson. (2010). *50 successful Harvard application essays: What worked for them can help you get into the college of your choice* (3rd ed.). New York: St. Martin's Griffin.

The Harvard Independent. (2002). *100 successful college application essays* (2nd ed.). New York: New American Library.

Heath, S. B. (1983). *Ways with words: Language, life, and work in communities and classrooms*. Cambridge, MA: Cambridge University Press.

Hillocks, G., Jr. (1986). *Research on writing composition: New directions for teaching*. Urbana, IL: National Council of Teachers of English.

Hillocks, G., Jr. (2007). *Narrative writing: Learning a new model for teaching*. Portsmouth, NH: Heinemann.

Hillocks, G., Jr. (2008). Writing in secondary schools. In C. Bazerman (Ed.), *Handbook of research on writing: History, society, school, individual, text* (pp. 311–329). New York: Lawrence Erlbaum Associates/Taylor & Francis Group.

Hull, G., & Schultz, K. (2002). *School's out! Bridging out-of-school literacies with classroom practice*. New York: Teachers College Press.

Hyland, K. (2007). Genre pedagogy: Language, literacy and L2 writing instruction. *Journal of Second Language Writing, 16*(3), 148–164.

Johnson, T. S., Thomspson, L., Smagorinsky, P., & Fry, P. G. (2003). Learning to teach the five paragraph theme. *Research in the Teaching of English, 38*(2), 136–176.

Jordan, K. (2010, August). *Inequalities in college destination selectivity: The impact of cultural capital and college admissions preparations*. Paper presented at the annual meeting of the American Sociological Association, Atlanta, GA.

Kamberelis, G. (1999). Genre development and learning: Children writing stories, science reports, and poems. *Research in the Teaching of English, 33*(4), 403–460.

Kinloch, V. (2008). Power, politics, and pedagogies: Re-imagining students' right to their own language through democratic engagements. In J. C. Scott, D. Straker, & L. Katz (Eds.), *Affirming students' right to their own language: Bridging language policies to teaching practices* (pp. 85–98). New York: Routledge.

Kinloch, V. (2010a). *Harlem on our minds: Place, race, and the literacies of urban youth.* New York: Teachers College Press.

Kinloch, V. (2010b). "To be a traitor of Black English": Youth perceptions of language rights in an urban context. *Teachers College Record, 112*(1), 103–141.

Kinloch, V., & San Pedro, T. (forthcoming). The space between listening and storying: Foundations for Projects in Humanization (PiH). In D. Paris & M.T. Winn (Eds.), *Humanizing Research.* Thousand Oaks, CA: Sage Publications.

Kirkland, D. (2010). English(es) in urban contexts: Politics, pluralism, and possibilities. *English Education, 42*(3), 293–306.

Kohn, A. (1999). *The schools our children deserve: Moving beyond traditional classrooms and "tougher standards."* Boston: Houghton Mifflin.

Kong, A., & Fitch, E. (2002/2003). Using book clubs to engage culturally and linguistically diverse learners in reading, writing, and talking about books. *The Reading Teacher, 56*(4), 352–362.

Kroll, B. M. (1981). Developmental relationships between speaking and writing. In B. M. Kroll & R. J. Vann (Eds.), *Exploring speaking-writing relationships: Connections and contrasts* (pp. 32–54). Urbana, IL: National Council of Teachers of English.

Labov, W. (1972). *Language in the inner city.* Philadelphia: University of Pennsylvania Press.

Lamott, A. (1994). *Bird by bird: Some instructions on writing and life.* New York: Pantheon.

Lankshear, C., & Knobel, M. (2003). *New literacies: Changing knowledge and classroom learning.* Buckingham, United Kingdom: Open University Press.

Lareau, A. (2006, August). *Cultural capital and the transition to college: Unequal childhoods grown up.* Paper presented at the annual meeting of the American Sociological Association, Montreal, Canada.

Lareau, A., & Weininger, E. B. (2003). Cultural capital in educational research: A critical assessment. *Theory and Society, 32*(5/6), 567–606.

Marshall, C., & Rossman, G. B. (1999). *Designing qualitative research* (3rd ed.). Thousand Oaks, CA: Sage.

Martin, J. L. (1989). *Factual writing: Exploring and challenging social reality.* Oxford, United Kingdom: Oxford University Press.

McGinty, S. M. (2006). *The college application essay* (rev. ed.). New York: College Board.

Miller, C. R. (1984). Genre as social action. *Quarterly Journal of Speech, 70*(2), 151–167.

Moll, L. C., Amanti, C., Neff, D., & González, N. (1992). Funds of knowledge for teaching: Using a qualitative approach to connect homes and classrooms. *Theory into Practice, 31*(1), 132–141.

Moore, T., & Morton, J. (1999). Authenticity in the IELTS academic module writing text. In R. Tulloch (Ed.), *IELTS research reports* (Vol. 2, pp. 64–106). Canberra, Australia: IELTS Australia.

Morrell, E. (2007). *Critical literacy and urban youth: Pedagogies of access, dissent, and liberation*. New York: Routledge.

Morrell, E., & Duncan-Andrade, J. (2002). Promoting academic literacy with urban youth through engaging in hip-hop culture. *English Journal, 91*(6), 88–92.

National Assessment of Education Progress. (2009, July 21). *The nation's report card*. Retrieved December 1, 2011, from nationsreportcard.gov/reading_math_grade12_2005/s0206.asp

The National Association for College Admission Counseling (NACAC). (2008). *Report of the commission on the use of standardized tests in undergraduate admission*. Arlington, VA: National Association for College Admission Counseling. Retrieved December 5, 2011, from www.nacacnet.org/PublicationsResources/Research/Documents/TestingComission_FinalReport.pdf

National Center for Education Statistics. (2009). *Degree-granting institutions, by control and type of institution: Selected years, 1949–50 through 2008–09*. Retrieved December 12, 2011, from http://nces.ed.gov/programs/digest/d09/tables/dt09_265.asp

National Commission on Writing. (2006). Writing and school reform including the neglected "R" the need for a writing revolution. Retrieved June 18, 2012, from http://www.collegeboard.com/prod_downloads/writingcom/writing-school-reform-natl-comm-writing.pdf

National Council of Teachers of English. (2008). *The NCTE Position Statement: The NCTE definition of 21st century literacies*. Retrieved December 7, 2011, from http://www.ncte.org/positions/statements/21stcentdefinition

Newkirk, T. (1997). *The performance of self in student writing*. Portsmouth, NH: Heinemann-Boynton/Cook.

The New London Group. (1996). A pedagogy of multiliteracies: Designing social futures. *Harvard Educational Review*, 66, (1), pp.60–92.

Nieto, S. (2009). *Language, culture, and teaching: Critical perspectives for a new century* (2nd ed.). New York: Routledge.

No Child Left Behind Act of 2001, 20 U.S.C.A. § 6301 et seq.

Oakes, J., & Wells, A. S. (1998). Detracking for high student achievement. *Educational Leadership, 55*(6), 38–41.

Pajares, F. (2003). Self-efficacy beliefs, motivation, and achievement in writing: A review of the literature. *Reading and Writing Quarterly, 19*(2), 139–158.

Pajares, F., & Johnson, M. J. (1994). Confidence and competence in writing: The role of writing self-efficacy, outcome expectancy, and apprehension. *Research in the Teaching of English, 28*(3), 313–331.

Pajares, F., Johnson, M. J., & Usher, E. L. (2007). Sources of writing self-efficacy beliefs of elementary, middle, and high school students. *Research in the Teaching of English, 42*(1), 104–120.

Paris, D. (2009). "They're in my culture, they speak the same way": African American language in multiethnic high schools. *Harvard Educational Review, 79*(3), 428–448.

Paris, D. (2010). Texting identities: Lessons for classrooms from multiethnic youth space. *English Education, 42*(3), 278–292.

Paris, D. (2011a). "A friend who understand fully": Notes on humanizing research in a multiethnic youth community. *International Journal of Qualitative Studies in Education, 24*(2), 137–149.

Paris, D. (2011b). *Language across difference: Ethnicity, communication, and youth identities in changing urban schools*. New York: Cambridge University Press.

Paris, D., & Kirkland, D. (2011). "The consciousness of the verbal artist": Understanding vernacular literacies in digital and embodied spaces. In V. Kinloch (Ed.), *Urban literacies: Critical perspectives on language, learning, and community* (pp. 177–194). New York: Teachers College Press.

Patton, M. Q. (1990). *Qualitative evaluation and research methods* (2nd ed.). Newbury Park, CA: Sage.

Peshkin, A. (1988). In search of subjectivity—one's own. *Educational Researcher, 17*(7), 17–21.

Pope, D. C. (2001). *"Doing school": How we are creating a generation of stressed out, materialistic, and miseducated students*. New Haven, CT: Yale University Press.

Prior, P. (2006). A sociocultural theory of writing. In C. A. MacArthur, S. Graham, & J. Fitzgerald (Eds.), *The handbook of writing research* (pp. 54–66). New York: Guilford Press.

Purcell-Gates, V. (1996). Stories, coupons, and the TV guide: Relationships between home literacy experiences and emergent literacy knowledge. *Reading Research Quarterly, 31*(4), 406–428.

Purcell-Gates, V., Duke, N. K., & Martineau, J. A. (2007). Learning to read and write genre-specific text: Roles of authentic experience and explicit teaching. *Reading Research Quarterly, 42*(1), 8–45.

Ramanathan, V., & Kaplan, R. B. (2000). Genres, authors, discourse communities: Theory and application for L2 writers. *Journal of Second Language Writing, 9*(2), 171–192.

Rampton, B. (1998). Language crossing and the redefinition of reality. In P. Auer (Ed.), *Code switching in conversation: Language, interaction and identity* (pp. 290–317). London: Routledge.

Robb, L. (2010). *Teaching middle school writers*. Portsmouth, NH: Heinemann.

Rodriguez, G. M., & Cruz, L. (2009). The transition to college of English learner and undocumented immigrant students: Resource and policy implications. *Teachers College Record, 111*(10), 2385–2418.

Ruiz-de-Velasco, J., & Fix, M. (with Clewell, B. C.) (2000). *Overlooked and underserved: Immigrant students in U.S. secondary schools*. Washington, DC: Urban Institute.

Samway, K. D. (2006). *When English language learners write: Connecting research to practice*. Portsmouth, NH: Heinemann.

San Pedro, T. (2011). *Providing that "Spark to Know More" about ourselves: Implications of teaching Native American literature to Native American students*. Paper presented at the Annual Meeting of the American Educational Research Association, New Orleans, LA.

Schnoor, D. J. (2004). *"Sing it, um, say it, um, read it again!": Poetry and preschool children's meaning-making responses*. Unpublished doctoral dissertation, University of Virginia, Charlottesville.

Shagoury, R., & Power, B. M. (2003). *The art of classroom inquiry: A handbook for teacher-researchers* (rev. ed.). Portsmouth, NH: Heinemann.

Singer, J. (2006). *Stirring up justice: Writing & reading to change the world*. Portsmouth, NH: Heinemann.

Singer, J. (2007). Preparing students for life after high school: An interview writing project. In T. Newkirk & R. Kent (Eds.), *Teaching the neglected "R": Rethinking writing instruction in secondary classrooms* (pp. 198–213). Portsmouth, NH: Heinemann.

Singer, J., & Hubbard, R. (2003). Teaching from the heart: Guiding adolescent writers to literate lives. *Journal of Adolescent & Adult Literacy, 46*(4), 326–338.

Sipe, L. R., & Ghiso, M. P. (2004). Developing conceptual categories in classroom descriptive research: Some problems and possibilities. *Anthropology and Education Quarterly, 35*(4), 472–485.

Smagorinsky, P., Daigle, E. A., O'Donnell-Allen, C., & Bynum, S. (2010). Bullshit in academic writing: A protocol analysis of a high school senior's process of interpreting *Much Ado About Nothing*. *Research in the Teaching of English, 44*(4), 368–405.

Smitherman, G. (2006). *Word from the mother: Language and African Americans*. New York: Routledge.

Solorzano, D., & Yosso, T. (2002). Critical race methodology: Counter-storytelling as an analytical framework for education research. *Qualitative Inquiry, 8*(1), 23–44.

Spinuzzi, C. (2003). *Tracing genres through organizations: A sociocultural approach to information design*. Cambridge, MA: MIT Press.

Spradley, J. P. (1979). *The ethnographic interview*. London: Wadsworth Group/Thompson Learning.

Strauss, A., & Corbin, J. (1990). *Basics of qualitative research: Grounded theory procedures and techniques*. Newbury Park, CA: Sage.

Street, C. (2005). Funds of knowledge at work in the writing classroom. *Multicultural Education, 13*(2), 22–25.

Support our law enforcement and safe neighborhoods act. Arizona Senate Bill 1070. (2010). Retrieved April 25, 2012, from http://www.azleg.gov/legtext/49leg/2r/bills/sb1070s.pdf

Swales, J. M. (1990). *Genre analysis: English in academic and research settings*. Cambridge, United Kingdom: Cambridge University Press.

Taylor, D., & Dorsey-Gaines, C. (1988). *Growing up literate: Learning from inner-city families*. Portsmouth, NH: Heinemann.

UC Regents (2010). *Personal statement*. Retrieved March 16, 2012, from: http://www.universityofcalifornia.edu/admissions/how-to-apply/personal-statement/index.html

U.S. Census. (2010). *United States Census: It's in your hands*. Retrieved February 29, 2012, from: http://2010.census.gov/2010census

U.S. Census Bureau. (2012). *State and county quickfacts.* Retrieved April 23, 2012, from http://quickfacts.census.gov/qfd/states/04/0446000.html

U.S. Department of Education. Institute of Education Sciences. National Center for Education Statistics. The Nation's Report Card: Writing 2002, NCES 2003–529, by H. R. Persky, M. C. Daane, and Y. Jin. Washington, DC: 2003.

Usher, E. L., & Pajares, F. (2008). Sources of self-efficacy in school: Critical review of the literature and future directions. *Review of Educational Research, 78*(4), 751–796.

Valdes, G. (2001). *Learning and not learning English: Latino students in American public schools.* New York: Teachers College Press.

Werner, E. E., & Smith, R. S. (1992). *Overcoming the odds: High-risk children from birth to adulthood.* New York: Cornell University Press.

Wiggins, G. (2009). Making purpose and audience matter. *English Journal, 98*(5), 29–37.

Winn, M. T. (2011). *Girl time: Literacy, justice, and the school-to-prison pipeline.* New York: Teachers College Press.

Yancey, K. B. (2000). More than a matter of form: Genre and writing. In L. K. Shamoon, R. M. Howard, S. Jamieson, & R. Schwegler (Eds.), *Coming of age: The advanced writing curriculum* (pp. 87–93). Portsmouth, NH: Heinemann-Boynton/Cook.

Yeh, S. S., & Smart, S. (1998). Empowering education: Teaching argumentative writing to cultural minority middle-school students. *Research in the Teaching of English, 33*(1), 49–83.

Yosso, T. J. (2005). Whose culture has capital? A critical race theory discussion of community cultural wealth. *Race Ethnicity and Education, 8(1)*, 69–91.

Zimmerman, B., & Bandura, A. (1994). Impact of self-regulatory influences on writing course attainment. *American Education Research Journal, 31*(4), 845–862.

Index

About the Authors

Jessica Singer Early is an assistant professor of English education in the Department of English at Arizona State University and the director of the Central Arizona Writing Project, a site of the National Writing Project. She is a former high school English teacher from Portland, Oregon, and has worked extensively with adolescent writers and secondary English language arts teachers throughout the West and Southwest. Her work examines language and literacy practices in ethnically and linguistically diverse secondary English classrooms as well as the preparation of urban English teachers. Her first book, *Stirring up Justice* (Heinemann), is a classroom-based examination of a literacy curriculum revolving around issues of activism within the secondary English classroom. Additionally, her research has been published in numerous journals, including *Bilingual Research Journal, Journal of Writing Research, Journal of Adolescent & Adult Literacy, Educational Leadership, Journal of Teaching and Teacher Education*, and *Rethinking Schools*. Jessica provides professional development programs on teaching writing in ethnically and linguistically diverse classrooms and on teaching real world and gate-opening writing to secondary students.

Meredith DeCosta received her Ph.D. in English education from Arizona State University. She taught English language arts at a high school in southern Indiana and is a teaching fellow of the Louisville Writing Project. She has co-authored several articles in journals such as *English Journal, Journal of Adolescent & Adult Literacy, NCTE's Classroom Notes Plus*, and *Educational Leadership*. She is currently the account manager of 1Love.org, a charitable giving platform established by the family of Bob Marley, and she teaches writing courses at Arizona State University.